THE QUIZ BOOK COMPANY

First published in 2004 by
The Quiz Book Company Ltd
Bardfield Centre,
Great Bardfield, Essex, CM7 4SL

2 4 6 8 10 9 7 5 3 1

ISBN 1-84236-500-2

Printed in India

Questions written by Chris Rigby.

QUIZ 1

• •

Whose reputed last words were…

1   CR "So little done, so much to do"?

2   JC "Et tu Brute"?

3   FDR "I have a terrific headache"?

4   PB "How were the circus receipts in Madison Square Gardens"?

5   EF "I've had a hell of a lot of fun and I've enjoyed every minute of it"?

6   PP "Drink to me"

7   OW "I am dying as I lived. Beyond my means"?

8   CD "I am not the least afraid to die"?

9   HB "I should never have switched from Scotch to Martinis"?

10 KM "Last words are for fools who haven't said enough"?

ANSWERS

1. Cecil Rhodes 2. Julius Caesar 3. Franklin D Roosevelt 4. Phineus Barnum
5. Errol Flynn 6. Pablo Picasso 7. Oscar Wilde 8. Charles Darwin
9. Humphrey Bogart 10. Karl Marx

QUIZ 2

• •

1 Who is the villainous counterpart of Dr Jekyll?

2 Where can Washington, Lincoln, Jefferson and Roosevelt be viewed in close proximity?

3 Who accompanied Sir Edmund Hillary to the peak of Everest in 1953?

4 In the 1960s which footballer acquired the nickname of "El Beatle"?

5 What is Superman's home planet?

6 By which title is Richard Bingham better known?

7 What is the name of Robin Hood's minstrel?

8 Who is the only British commoner to have been granted a state funeral?

9 At the siege of Troy, who killed Achilles?

10 Which country includes William Tell among its national heroes?

ANSWERS

1. Mr Hyde 2. Mount Rushmore 3. Sherpa Tenzing Norgay 4. George Best
5. Krypton 6. Lord Lucan 7. Alan-a-Dale 8. Diana, Princess of Wales 9. Paris
(with an arrow guided by Apollo) 10. Switzerland

QUIZ 3

• •

1 Which crime series featured a villain called Wo Fat?

2 Who played the role of Robert McCall in *The Equaliser*?

3 Who was the first actor to play Dr Who on TV?

4 By what collective name were the TV heroes Brett Sinclair and Danny Wilde known?

5 What is the character name of the Bionic Man, played by Lee Majors?

6 Westbridge is the home town of which teenage witch?

7 Sergeant Joe Friday is the lead character in which series?

8 What is the home town of Buffy the Vampire Slayer?

9 In *Thunderbirds*, what is the name of Lady Penelope's chauffeur?

10 In which city did Kojak bring criminals to justice?

ANSWERS

1. Hawaii 5-0 2. Edward Woodward 3. William Hartnell 4. *The Persuaders*
5. Steve Austin 6. Sabrina 7. Dragnet 8. Sunnydale 9. Parker 10. New York

QUIZ 4

• •

1 Who played the role of George Carter in *The Sweeney*?

2 In which series did Pete Duel and Ben Murphy play the Wild West outlaws Hannibal Heyes and Kid Curry?

3 Which conflict saw the war hero Richard Sharpe battling against the French?

4 Who played the role of Templeton Peck in *The A Team*?

5 Who drove a car called the General Lee?

6 In which series does James Gandolfini play a New Jersey Mafia boss?

7 Who created *Inspector Morse*?

8 On TV, who has played the roles of Oz, Jed and Spender?

9 What is the name of the character played by David Duchovny in *The X Files*?

10 Who played the title role in *Bergerac*?

ANSWERS

1. Dennis Waterman 2. *Alias Smith And Jones* 3. Napoleonic War 4. Dirk Benedict 5. *The Dukes Of Hazzard* 6. *The Sopranos* 7. Colin Dexter 8. Jimmy Nail 9. Fox Mulder 10. John Nettles

QUIZ 5

• •

1   Who killed one thousand Philistines with the jawbone of an ass?

2   Who was the leader of the Israelite army at the Battle of Jericho?

3   What is the name of the mother of John the Baptist?

4   Which Biblical king is represented by the king of spades in a pack of cards?

5   Who, in the Bible, killed 25 percent of the world's population?

6   Which king of Babylon destroyed Jerusalem in the second book of Kings?

7   In the Bible which witch raised the spirit of Samuel?

8   Who was the thief released by Pontius Pilate in place of Jesus?

9   In the Old Testament, which wife of King Ahab was eaten by dogs?

10 In the New Testament, who is known as The Beloved Physician?

ANSWERS

1. Samson 2. Joshua 3. Elizabeth 4. King David 5. Cain 6. Nebuchadnezzar
II 7. The Witch of Endor 8. Barabbas 9. Jezebel 10. Luke

QUIZ 6

• •

1 By which one-word name is Rebecca Rolfe better known?

2 What was the name of Roy Rogers' dog?

3 Who is the patron saint of Germany?

4 Who was the first woman to be elected into the Country and Western Hall of Fame in the USA?

5 According to the Ian Fleming novels, in which decade was James Bond born?

6 Which Polish electrician won the 1983 Nobel Peace Prize?

7 Which US hero owned a rifle called Old Betsy?

8 *Leader* is the title of the autobiography of which former pop star?

9 Who was the last inmate of Spandau Prison?

10 Who was the Archbishop of Canterbury, when his envoy Terry Waite was kidnapped?

ANSWERS

1. Pocahontas 2. Bullet 3. St Boniface 4. Patsy Cline 5. 1920s 6. Lech Walesa
7. Davy Crockett 8. Gary Glitter 9. Rudolph Hess 10. Robert Runcie

QUIZ 7

• •

1   Who created Adrian Mole?

2   Cardinal Richelieu is the archenemy of which literary trio?

3   Which literary sleuth is assisted by Captain Hastings?

4   Who created the character of Huckleberry Finn?

5   In *Treasure Island,* what is the name of Long John Silver's parrot?

6   Who did Sherlock Holmes refer to as the Napoleon of Crime?

7   Which novel introduced the bullying character of Flashman?

8   How is the literary hero Sir Percy Blakeney otherwise known?

9   What is the first name of Miss Marple?

10 Which Daniel Defoe character spent 24 years marooned on a desert island?

ANSWERS

1. Sue Townsend 2. The Three Musketeers 3. Hercule Poirot 4. Mark Twain
5. Captain Flint 6. Professor Moriaty 7. *Tom Brown's Schooldays*
8. The Scarlet Pimpernel 9. Jane 10. Robinson Crusoe

QUIZ 8

1 In which city was Dick Turpin executed?

2 Which Dutch dancer was executed for spying by the French in 1917?

3 In which county was Sir Walter Raleigh born?

4 By what name is the pirate Edward Teach better known?

5 Which painter, born in 1887, worked as an employee of the *Manchester Guardian*?

6 What was the name of Alfred the Great's kingdom?

7 Who published his theory of relativity in 1905?

8 Who was the mother of Queen Elizabeth I?

9 Which decade witnessed the death of General George Custer?

10 In what year was Captain James Cook killed by Hawaiian natives?

ANSWERS

1. York 2. Mata Hari 3. Devon 4. Blackbeard 5. LS Lowry 6. Wessex 7. Albert Einstein 8. Anne Boleyn 9. 1870s 10. 1779

QUIZ 9

• •

1 Who played the Prime Minister of Great Britain in the 2003 film comedy, *Love Actually*?

2 In which 1987 film did Michael Douglas play a ruthless stockbroker called Gordon Gekko?

3 Who played the evil fiancé of Kate Winslet in *Titanic*?

4 Which film hero has the middle name of Dangerous?

5 Which was the first film to feature the cannibalistic character of Hannibal Lecter?

6 In which 2003 film did Sean Connery play the role of Allan Quartermain?

7 Who played the husband of Gwyneth Paltrow in the film *Seven*?

8 Who exchanged identities with John Travolta in the action movie *Face Off*?

9 Who played the wife of Gary Cooper in *High Noon*?

10 Which political activist was portrayed by Mario Van Peebles in the film *Ali*?

ANSWERS

1. Hugh Grant 2. *Wall Street* 3. Billy Zane 4. Austin Powers 5. *Manhunter*
6. *The League Of Extraordinary Gentlemen* 7. Brad Pitt 8. Nicholas Cage
9. Grace Kelly 10. Malcolm X

QUIZ 10

. . . .

1 What is the real first name of Indiana Jones?

2 Tatooine is the home planet of which *Star Wars* hero?

3 Who played the title role in the 1960 movie epic *Spartacus*?

4 Who provided the voice of Woody in *Toy Story*?

5 In which film did Peter O'Toole play T.E. Lawrence?

6 In the second *Star Trek* movie, the crew of the *Enterprise* incurred the wrath of which villain?

7 Who has played Crocodile Dundee in three films?

8 What kind of animal is Sebastian in the Disney film *The Little Mermaid*?

9 In which film did Richard Dreyfuss play a reluctant hero called Roy Neary?

10 Who played Robin Hood in the film *Time Bandits*?

ANSWERS

1. Henry 2. Luke Skywalker 3. Kirk Douglas 4. Tom Hanks 5. *Lawrence Of Arabia* 6. Khan 7. Paul Hogan 8. Crab 9. *Close Encounters Of The Third Kind* 10. John Cleese

QUIZ 11

1. Who did Richard Attenborough chillingly portray in the film *10, Rilington Place*?

2. Who acquired the nickname of the Oklahoma Bomber?

3. Who was the FBI's first Public Enemy Number 1?

4. Who was the last woman to be hanged in Britain?

5. Who did John Hinckley attempt to assassinate in 1981?

6. Which film star was John Hinckley trying to impress in his assassination bid?

7. Who tied the knot with Roberta Jones in Maidstone Prison in 1997?

8. Who was found not guilty of the murder of Ronald Goldman?

9. What was the surname of Bonnie with regard to *Bonnie and Clyde*?

10. What was the surname of Clyde with regard to *Bonnie and Clyde*?

ANSWERS

1. John Christie 2. Timothy McVeigh 3. John Dillinger 4. Ruth Ellis 5. Ronald Reagan 6. Jodie Foster 7. Reggie Kray 8. OJ Simpson 9. Parker 10. Barrow

QUIZ 12

. . . .

1 Who was the first footballer to receive a knighthood?

2 Which Spanish king celebrated his Silver Jubilee in 2000?

3 Which Stephen Sondheim musical tells the story of a murderous barber?

4 Which pop hero left the Crickets to forge a solo career?

5 Whose two-volume autobiography is entitled *I Am Not Spock and I Am Spock*?

6 Who acquired the nickname of The Father Of The Modern Computer?

7 What is the home city of the movie star Jean Claude Van Damme?

8 In which decade was the dictator Idi Amin born?

9 To which saint is the cathedral in Moscow's Red Square dedicated?

10 For which football club did Bobby Charlton play his last league game?

ANSWERS

1. Sir Stanley Matthews 2. King Juan Carlos 3. Sweeney Todd 4. Buddy
Holly 5. Leonard Nimoy 6. Charles Babbage 7. Brussels 8. 1920s 9. St Basil
10. Preston North End

QUIZ 13

• •

1 In *Thunderbirds*, which island is home to the headquarters of International Rescue?

2 In which series does Kiefer Sutherland play CTU operative Jack Bauer?

3 By what colourful name is the TV hero Paul Metcalfe better known?

4 Which actor achieved international recognition after landing the role of James T Kirk?

5 Which is the home town of Fireman Sam?

6 What is the last name of Buffy the Vampire Slayer?

7 Who played the role of Tara King in *The Avengers*?

8 Which US series, set in Los Angeles, featured two motorcycle cops called Ponch and Jonathan?

9 What is the first name of Cagney in *Cagney And Lacey*?

10 Who played the role of Blake in the sci-fi series *Blake's Seven*?

ANSWERS

1. Tracy Island 2. 24 3. Captain Scarlet 4. William Shatner 5. Pontypandy
6. Summers 7. Linda Thorson 8. CHIPS 9. Christine 10. Gareth Thomas

QUIZ 14

. . . .

Identify the actors who play the title role in the
 following series:

1 *Jonathan Creek*

2 *Judge John Deed*

3 *Xena Warrior Princess*

4 *McCloud*

5 *Sabrina The Teenage Witch*

6 *Hetty Wainthropp Investigates*

7 *Boon*

8 *Magnum PI*

9 *The Rockford Files*

10 *Shoestring*

ANSWERS

1. Alan Davies 2. Martin Shaw 3. Lucy Lawless 4. Dennis Weaver 5. Melissa
Joan Hart 6. Patricia Routledge 7. Michael Elphick 8. Tom Selleck 9. James
Garner 10. Trevor Eve

QUIZ 15

1 Steve Rogers is the secret identity of which superhero?

2 Which newspaper does Clark Kent, alias Superman, work for?

3 Which superhero brought justice to the streets of Mega City One?

4 In which country was the series *Supergran* set?

5 Who does Dr Banner turn into when he loses his temper?

6 Who does Dr Blake turn into when he bangs his hammer?

7 Eric the schoolboy is the secret identity of which fruity superhero?

8 Who played the role of Batgirl in the 1997 film *Batman And Robin*?

9 What is the name of the superhero played by Ardal O'Hanlon in the TV comedy series *My Hero*?

10 Who played the title role in the 1984 film *Supergirl*?

ANSWERS

1. Captain America 2. *Daily Planet* 3. Judge Dredd 4. Scotland
5. The Incredible Hulk 6. The Mighty Thor 7. Bananaman 8. Alicia
Silverstone 9. Thermoman 10. Helen Slater

QUIZ 16

. . . .

1 Which Arsenal defender scored England's first goal in the 2002 World Cup finals?

2 Which Roman emperor gave his name to the chief river that runs through Rome?

3 Which king sealed the Magna Carta?

4 Who succeeded the assassinated US president Abraham Lincoln?

5 By what name is the pickpocket Jack Dawkins better known?

6 What was the nationality of Oskar Schindler, of *Schindler's List* fame?

7 Which US political party does Arnold Schwarzenegger represent?

8 What is the name of the mother of the pantomime hero Aladdin?

9 Which composer replaced Michael Faraday on the back of a £20 note?

10 By what name is Karol Wojtyla better known?

ANSWERS

1. Sol Campbell 2. Tiberius 3. King John 4. Andrew Johnson 5. The Artful Dodger 6. Austrian 7. Republican 8. Widow Twanky 9. Edward Elgar 10. Pope John Paul II

QUIZ 17

• •

1   Who created the character of Captain Nemo?

2   Which employee of Hogwarts School owns a pet dog called Fang?

3   Which title character of a controversial novel is the mistress of Radley Hall?

4   Which literary heroine marries Mr Rochester?

5   Who raised an orphaned lion cub called Elsa, then wrote of her exploits in the book *Born Free*?

6   Emma Harte is the heroine of which 20th-century, best-selling novel?

7   Passepartout is the name of the servant of which globe-trotting character?

8   What is the name of the hero of the novel *Kidnapped*?

9   Which British boxer penned an autobiography entitled *Zero To Hero*?

10 In *The Lord Of The Rings*, Glamdring is the name of Gandalf's what?

ANSWERS

QUIZ 18

• •

1   Who founded the Metropolian Police Force?

2   Who married Philip Mountbatten in 1947?

3   Which British military hero was once quoted as saying, "Publish and be damned"?

4   In 1721, who became the first prime minister of Great Britain?

5   In what decade did King George VI die?

6   Which Russian tsar died in 1725, to be succeeded by his wife Catherine?

7   Was Sir Isaac Newton born in Lancashire, Lincolnshire or Leicestershire?

8   In 1070, who led a Saxon revolt in East Anglia?

9   Which Frenchman was the first person to fly over the English Channel?

10 Which famed scientist declined the presidency of Israel in 1952?

ANSWERS

1. Robert Peel 2. Princess Elizabeth (later Queen Elizabeth II) 3. Duke of Wellington 4. Sir Robert Walpole 5. 1950s 1952 6. Peter the Great 7. Lincolnshire 8. Hereward the Wake 9. Louis Blériot 10. Albert Einstein

QUIZ 19

• •

1 Who played Kelly in the film *Kelly's Heroes*?

2 What is the first name of the character played by Patrick Swayze in the film *Ghost*?

3 What is the first name of the character played by Demi Moore in the film *Ghost*?

4 In which film did Mel Gibson play the role of Colonel Benjamin Martin?

5 Which actor romanced Julia Roberts in *Pretty Woman*?

6 In which film did Julie Andrews sing 'Feed The Birds'?

7 When Errol Flynn played the hero Robin Hood, which villain was played by Basil Rathbone?

8 In 2003, who received her thirteenth Oscar nomination?

9 Atticus Finch is the name of the hero in which film and novel?

10 Which of Dorothy's three companions in *The Wizard Of Oz* was played by Bert Lahr?

ANSWERS

1. Clint Eastwood 2. Sam 3. Molly 4. *The Patriot* 5. Richard Gere 6. Mary Poppins 7. Guy of Gisbourne 8. Meryl Streep 9. *To Kill A Mockingbird* 10. Cowardly Lion

QUIZ 20

• •

1 Which rock star played the outlaw Ned Kelly in a 1970 film?

2 In how many films did Carrie Fisher play the role of Princess Leia?

3 Who played the title role in the 1992 film *Passenger 57*?

4 Who played the title role in the comedy film *Carry On Dick*?

5 In which film did Roy Scheider play the heroic figure of Chief Martin Brody?

6 Who played the boxer Clubber Lang in *Rocky III*?

7 Which heroine returned to the big screen in a film sequel subtitled *The Cradle Of Life*?

8 In which country was the actor Russell Crowe born?

9 Which villain, played in several films by Gene Hackman, terrorized the city of Metropolis?

10 Who did Alan Rickman play in *Robin Hood Prince Of Thieves*?

ANSWERS

1. Mick Jagger 2. Three 3. Wesley Snipes 4. Sid James 5. *Jaws* 6. Mr T
7. Lara Croft 8. New Zealand 9. Lex Luthor 10. The Sheriff of Nottingham

QUIZ 21

• •

1 By what beastly nickname is the terrorist Ilich Ramirez Sanchez otherwise known?

2 What nickname was acquired by the gangster Salvatore Luciano in 1929?

3 In which country was Osama Bin Laden born?

4 In which city did Burke and Hare steal bodies for Doctor Knox?

5 Which author of *The Importance Of Being Earnest* was jailed for two years in 1895?

6 In 2001, which lord and multi-millionaire author was sentenced to prison for perjury?

7 Whose gang members were slaughtered in the 1929 St Valentine's Day Massacre?

8 Who was found guilty in his absence for the murder of nanny Sandra Rivett?

9 What is the name of the Yorkshire Ripper?

10 Who died at sea in November 1991, after falling from a yacht called the Lady Ghislaine?

ANSWERS

1. Carlos the Jackal 2. Lucky 3. Saudi Arabia 4. Edinburgh 5. Oscar Wilde
6. Jeffrey Archer 7. Bugs Moran 8. Lord Lucan 9. Peter Sutcliffe 10. Robert Maxwell

QUIZ 22

• •

1　During which war of the 1980s did Prince Andrew see active service?

2　Who is the oldest of the Osmond Brothers?

3　What colour shirts did England wear when they beat West Germany in the 1966 World Cup final?

4　In which country was Bob Marley granted a state funeral?

5　Which fictional sleuth lives at 698, Candlewood Lane, Cabot Cove, Maine?

6　Which former British prime minister was made a Companion of Honour in the 1999 honours list?

7　Who managed Manchester United to European Cup glory in 1968?

8　In Arthurian legend, whose sword was called Arondight?

9　Which US astronaut relayed the message back to Earth "Houston we have a problem"?

10　What is the name of the character played by Michael J Fox in the *Back To The Future* film trilogy?

ANSWERS

1.Falklands War 2.Alan 3.Red 4.Jamaica 5.Jessica Fletcher 6.John Major
7.Sir Matt Busby 8.Sir Lancelot 9.Jim Lovell 10.Marty McFly

QUIZ 23

• •

1 Which race of aliens is the archenemy of Captain Scarlet?

2 In which TV drama does Robbie Coltrane play the psychologist Eddie Fitzgerald?

3 In which sitcom did Richard Gibson play a German villain called Herr Flick?

4 Who is the captain of Pippin Fort at Camberwick Green?

5 In which series did Nicholas Lyndhurst travel through time as Gary Sparrow?

6 Who played Jonathan Hart in *Hart To Hart*?

7 Which Roman emperor was portrayed by John Hurt in *I Claudius*?

8 Which British actor plays Rupert Giles in *Buffy The Vampire Slayer*?

9 Which 1960s TV show starring Bill Cosby was adapted into a 21st-century film starring Eddie Murphy?

10 What name connects the heroes in *M.A.S.H.* and *Last Of The Mohicans*?

ANSWERS

1. Mysterons 2. *Cracker* 3. *Allo Allo* 4. Captain Flack 5. *Goodnight Sweetheart*
6. Robert Wagner 7. Caligula 8. Anthony Head 9. *I Spy* 10. Hawkeye

QUIZ 24

1 Which jungle dweller was played by Ron Ely in a 1960s TV series?

2 Who replaced Tom Baker as Dr Who?

3 Which car is driven by both Arthur Daley and Inspector Morse?

4 Which compatriot of the Lone Ranger rides a horse called Scout?

5 Which police officer is the chief adversary of Top Cat?

6 In which series does John Nettles play DCI Barnaby?

7 Which series saw the heroic character of Mike Donovan battling against reptilian aliens?

8 Who played the role of Gambit in *The New Avengers*?

9 Which organization did Mr Waverley and Napoleon Solo work for?

10 Cigarette Smoking Man is the name of a villain in which TV series?

ANSWERS

1. Tarzan 2. Peter Davison 3. Jaguar 4. Tonto 5. Officer Dibble 6. *Midsomer Murders* 7. *V* 8. Gareth Hunt 9. U.N.C.L.E. 10. *The X Files*

QUIZ 25

1 How is the Gotham City villain Jack Napier better known?

2 How is the Gotham City villain Oswald Cobblepot better known?

3 Skeletor is the archenemy of which superhero?

4 On which island was the TV crime drama *Bergerac* set?

5 The Mekon is the archenemy of which space-age hero?

6 What title is held by Ming the Merciless, the archenemy of Flash Gordon?

7 Which super villain was played by Willem Dafoe in the big screen version of *Spiderman*?

8 Which Swedish actor played Ming the Merciless in the 1980 film *Flash Gordon*?

9 Which foe of Spiderman has eight robotic arms?

10 The Red Skull is the archenemy of which superhero?

ANSWERS

1. The Joker 2. The Penguin 3. He Man 4. Jersey 5. Dan Dare
6. Emperor 7. The Green Goblin 8. Max von Sydow 9. Dr Octopus
10. Captain America

QUIZ 26

• •

1 Traditionally, witches hold their meetings on which night of the week?

2 Which Rovers does Roy of the Rovers play for?

3 Which Shakespeare king announced, "Now is the winter of our discontent"?

4 At what age did Marilyn Monroe die?

5 What is the home town of Tom Sawyer?

6 In which country was Pope John Paul II born?

7 Ice skaters Torvill and Dean were both created freemen of which English city?

8 Whose followers became known as The 26th Of July Movement?

9 Who died before he could stand trial for the murder of Nancy Spungen?

10 Who was the first woman to swim 100m in under one minute?

ANSWERS

QUIZ 27

• •

Which Dickens novel features a …

1 clerk called Bob Cratchit?

2 undertaker called Mr Sowerberry?

3 convict called Abel Magwitch?

4 cricketer called Mr Dumkins?

5 schoolteacher called Bradley Headstone?

6 crooked lawyer called Sampson Brass?

7 surveyor called Seth Pecksniff?

8 school headmaster called Mr Creakle?

9 mill owner called Thomas Gradgrind?

10 executioner called Ned Dennis?

ANSWERS

1. *A Christmas Carol* 2. *Oliver Twist* 3. *Great Expectations* 4. *The Pickwick Papers* 5. *Our Mutual Friend* 6. *The Old Curiosity Shop* 7. *Martin Chuzzlewitt* 8. *David Copperfield* 9. *Hard Times* 10. *Barnaby Rudge*

QUIZ 28

. . . .

1   In which year did Richard Nixon resign his
    presidency?

2   In which month of the year was John F Kennedy
    assassinated?

3   Which part of his anatomy did Horatio Nelson
    lose at the Battle of Santa Cruz?

4   Which king's son was nicknamed The Black
    Prince?

5   Which queen travelled to Jerusalem to test the
    wisdom of Solomon?

6   Who died attempting to beat his own world
    record on Coniston Water in January 1967?

7   Who was the first woman to receive the Order of
    the Merit?

8   Who led the Mutiny on the Bounty?

9   Westminster Abbey is dedicated to which saint?

10 Who was president of South Africa when Nelson
    Mandela was released from jail in 1990?

ANSWERS

1. 1974 2. November 3. Right arm 4. Edward III 5. The Queen of Sheba
6. Donald Campbell 7. Florence Nightingale 8. Fletcher Christian 9. St Peter
10. FW De Klerk

QUIZ 29

. . . .

1 In which Bond movie did Sean Connery appear alongside Kim Basinger?

2 In which film did Alan Rickman play a terrorist called Hans Gruber?

3 Who plays Dr Banner in the 2003 film *Hulk*?

4 In which 1996 film did John Travolta play an angel?

5 In which film did Demi Moore shave her head and join the ranks of the Navy Seals?

6 In *The Magnificent Seven* who played Chris, the leader of the seven?

7 In which 1987 film was Michael Douglas stalked by Glenn Close?

8 Who played the young Indiana Jones in *Indiana Jones And The Last Crusade*?

9 Who played the role of Bonnie in the 1967 film *Bonnie And Clyde*?

10 Who played the role of Clyde in the 1967 film *Bonnie And Clyde*?

ANSWERS

1. *Never Say Never Again* 2. *Die Hard* 3. Eric Bana 4. *Michael* 5. *GI Jane*
6. Yul Brynner 7. *Fatal Attraction* 8. River Phoenix 9. Faye Dunaway
10. Warren Beatty

QUIZ 30

. . . .

1 Which actor played the role of Norman Bates in several films?

2 Which Swedish-born filmstar played the title role in the 1948 film *Joan of Arc*?

3 Which serial killer was the subject of the films *A Study In Terror* and *From Hell*?

4 Which horror movie veteran played the evil sorceror Sarumen in *The Lord Of The Rings* trilogy?

5 Who portrayed Mrs James Bond in *On Her Majesty's Secret Service*?

6 Which London square is home to a statue of Charlie Chaplin?

7 Which series of horror flicks features a murderous doll called Chucky?

8 Which series of horror flick features a hideous villain called Pinhead?

9 Who played the black hearted General Zod in *Superman II*?

10 Which movie icon acquired the nickname of The King of Hollywood?

ANSWERS

1. Anthony Perkins 2. Ingrid Bergman 3. Jack the Ripper 4. Christopher Lee
5. Diana Rigg 6. Leicester Square 7. *Child's Play* 8. *Hellraiser* 9. Terence
Stamp 10. Clark Gable

QUIZ 31

• •

1 In which city did Al Capone operate?

2 In which decade was the Australian outlaw Ned Kelly hanged?

3 Which killer was nicknamed the French Bluebeard?

4 Which Bond movie featured a smuggler called Columbo?

5 Which associate of the Kray twins was nicknamed The Hat?

6 Which outlaw was born Robert Leroy Parker?

7 Who became known as the Robin Hood of Texas?

8 Who formed the Quantrill Gang with his brother Jesse?

9 From which prison did the train robber Ronnie Biggs escape?

10 What nickname was bestowed upon the killer Joseph Smith?

ANSWERS

1. Chicago 2. 1880s 3. Henri Landru 4. *For Your Eyes Only* 5. Jack The Hat McVitie 6. Butch Cassidy 7. Sam Bass 8. Frank James 9. Wandsworth
10. The Brides In The Bath Murderer

QUIZ 32

. . . .

1   Who was the first footballer to win 100 caps for England?

2   Who was born Agatha May Clarissa Miller?

3   Who was protected by a shield called Pridwen?

4   Which great composer was born in Bonn in 1770 and died in Vienna in 1827?

5   The wife of which South American dictator died of cancer in 1952?

6   Which leader said "Veni, vidi, vici"?

7   Who was born on the island of Corsica in 1769 and went on to become known as The Man of Destiny?

8   How were Frank Sinatra, Joey Bishop, Dean Martin, Peter Lawford and Sammy Davis Jnr collectively known?

9   Who was World Figure Skating Champion four times in the 1980s?

10 Who was the first Pope?

ANSWERS

1. Billy Wright 2. Agatha Christie 3. King Arthur 4. Ludwig Van Beethoven
5. Eva Peron 6. Julius Caesar 7. Napoleon Bonaparte 8. The Rat Pack
9. Katrina Witt 10. St Peter

QUIZ 33

1 Who played Ilya Kuryakin in *The Man From U.N.C.L.E.*?

2 Which character was portrayed by Joanna Lumley in *The New Avengers*?

3 Which government department did Bodie and Doyle work for in *The Professionals*?

4 Who played Jesus in the TV mini series *Jesus Of Nazareth*?

5 Which doctor travels through time in the sci-fi series *Quantum Leap*?

6 Lieutenant Worf and Commander Ryker have both served on which vessel?

7 Who plays the title role in *Lovejoy*?

8 Which of the Wombles was named after the world's most southerly capital city?

9 What is the first name of the Leslie Charteris creation *The Saint*?

10 What is the last name of Charlie in *Charlie's Angels*?

ANSWERS

QUIZ 34

. . . .

1. In which series did Nicholas Lyndhurst play a hapless spy called Peter Chapman?

2. Which Addams' family uncle was played by Jackie Coogan?

3. On TV, who played the anti-hero Yosser Hughes?

4. Who performed the theme for *The Dukes Of Hazzard*?

5. Which puppet series features the character of Commander Shore?

6. Which TV character left Sunshine Desserts to set up a business empire called Grot?

7. How is the cartoon superhero Prince Adam better known?

8. Who portrayed the Man of Steel in *The New Adventures of Superman*?

9. What is the name of Michael Knight's car in *Knight Rider*?

10. Which female detective played on TV by Patricia Hodge was created by Antonia Fraser?

ANSWERS

1. *The Piglet Files* 2. Uncle Fester 3. Bernard Hill 4. Waylon Jennings
5. *Stingray* 6. Reginald Perrin 7. He Man 8. Dean Cain 9. KITT 10. Jemima Shore

QUIZ 35

• •

1 What is the name of the policeman in the Noddy stories?

2 In *Miami Vice*, which detective owns a pet alligator called Elvis?

3 In which TV series did Michael Douglas play Californian cop Steve Keller?

4 Who was the first woman to be appointed head of MI5?

5 Which streetwise cop was played by Gene Hackman in *The French Connection*?

6 In which TV series did Patrick Malahide play Inspector Chisholm?

7 Which bumbling inspector was portrayed by Peter Sellers in the *Pink Panther* movies?

8 Who played Mary Beth Lacey in *Cagney And Lacey*?

9 In which decade was London's Metropolitan police founded?

10 In which series does Dennis Franz play Detective Andy Sipowicz?

ANSWERS

1. PC Plod 2. Sonny Crockett 3. *The Streets Of San Francisco* 4. Stella Rimington 5. Popeye Doyle 6. *Minder* 7. Inspector Clouseau 8. Tyne Daly 9. 1820s 10. *NYPD Blue*

QUIZ 36

• •

1 Which swimmer won six gold medals at the 2002 Commonwealth Games?

2 Who led the Argonauts in their quest for the Golden Fleece?

3 In which country was Adolf Hitler born?

4 Who was Britain's first million-pound footballer?

5 In the Bible, Goliath was a member of which tribe of people?

6 Which female tennis star is nicknamed the Swiss Miss?

7 What is the legendary King Arthur's last name?

8 Which high-kicking heroine holds the title of Duchess of St Bridget?

9 Who played the role of Rick in the classic movie *Casablanca*?

10 In the Bible, which sea did Moses part the waves of?

ANSWERS

1. Ian Thorpe 2. Jason 3. Austria 4. Trevor Francis 5. Philistines 6. Martina Hingis 7. Pendragon 8. Lara Croft 9. Humphrey Bogart 10. The Red Sea

QUIZ 37

· ·

1　What is the last name of Harry Potter's evil Uncle Vernon?

2　Who plays Mrs Weasley in the *Harry Potter* movies?

3　Which house is attended by the mean-spirited Draco Malfoy?

4　What is the name of Draco Malfoy's evil father?

5　Which professor attempted to steal the Philosopher's Stone while possessed by Lord Voldermort?

6　Which hapless wizard lost his memory in *Harry Potter And The Chamber Of Secrets*?

7　Who was killed by Bellatrix Lestrange in the fifth *Harry Potter* novel?

8　What type of creature killed Moaning Myrtle?

9　Which Hogwart's hero is played on film by Robbie Coltrane?

10　Who owns a pet phoenix called Fawkes?

ANSWERS

1. Dursley 2. Julie Walters 3. Slytherin 4. Lucius 5. Professor Quirrel
6. Gilderoy Lockhart 7. Sirius Black 8. Snake 9. Hagrid
10. Albus Dumbledore

QUIZ 38

. . . .

1 In which state of the USA did Davy Crockett die?

2 Which fruit is associated with the alternative name of King William III?

3 In 1850, who established the world's first detective agency?

4 Who led an historic voyage in the Santa Maria in 1492?

5 Who was the train driver of the *Cannonball Express*?

6 How is the outlaw William H Bonney better known?

7 Which fictional character was inspired by Vlad the Impaler?

8 Who married Mary Todd in November 1842?

9 In which cemetery is Karl Marx buried?

10 Who was king of England during World War II?

ANSWERS

1. Texas 2. Orange (William of Orange) 3. Allan Pinkerton 4. Christopher Columbus 5. Casey Jones 6. Billy the Kid 7. Dracula 8. Abraham Lincoln 9. Highgate 10. King George VI

QUIZ 39

• •

1. Which FA Cup hero starred in the films *Snatch* and *Gone In 60 Seconds*?

2. In which series of films does Keanu Reeves play the role of Neo?

3. Who played the Manufacturer in *The Great Escape*?

4. Which 1991 film starred Kevin Costner investigating a 1963 assassination?

5. Who played Moses in the 1956 movie epic *The Ten Commandments*?

6. What is the name of the captain of the Orca in *Jaws*?

7. In which film did Robert Redford play a rodeo star called Sonny Steele?

8. What is the name of the character played by Clark Gable in *Gone With The Wind*?

9. What is Bert's job in *Mary Poppins*?

10. Which emperor was portrayed by Peter Ustinov in *Quo Vadis*?

ANSWERS

1. Vinnie Jones 2. *The Matrix* 3. James Coburn 4. *JFK* 5. Charlton Heston
6. Captain Quint 7. *The Electric Horseman* 8. Rhett Butler 9. Chimney sweep
10. Nero

QUIZ 40

• •

1 What were Marilyn Monroe's first two names at birth?

2 Which Blues Brother was memorably played on film by John Belushi?

3 How many *Death Wish* movies did Charles Bronson make?

4 Which film duo were accompanied to South America by Etta Place?

5 In which multi Oscar-winning film did Lieutenant John Dunbar befriend a dog called Two Socks?

6 Which actor was confined to a wheelchair in the 1954 Hitchcock thriller *Rear Window*?

7 Which 1995 film saw Susan Sarandon donning a wimple while comforting a death row convict?

8 In which film did Robin Williams play an unconventional teacher called John Keating?

9 Which artist was portrayed by Charlton Heston in the film *The Agony And The Ecstasy*?

10 In which film did a young Elizabeth Taylor play the role of Velvet Brown?

ANSWERS

1. Norma Jean 2. Jake 3. Five 4. Butch Cassidy and the Sundance Kid
5. *Dances With Wolves* 6. James Stewart 7. *Dead Man Walking* 8. *Dead Poets' Society* 9. Michelangelo 10. *National Velvet*

QUIZ 41

1 Which of the Kray twins died a free man?

2 Which female killer was immortalized in a rhyme that claimed that "she gave her mother forty whacks"?

3 What nickname was given to the serial killer Albert De Salvo?

4 Which Californian prison welcomed Al Capone as an inmate, after he was found guilty of tax evasion?

5 Which Moors murderer died in 2002?

6 Which duo were gunned down on May 23, 1934 in an ambush by Texas Rangers?

7 Which security warehouse at Heathrow airport was relieved of £26 million worth of gold bullion in 1983?

8 The film *Helter Skelter* told of which criminal's reign of terror and subsequent trial?

9 Bruno Hauptmann was executed in 1935 for the kidnap and murder of which aviator's baby son?

10 By what nickname was the gangster Jack Diamond otherwise known?

ANSWERS

1. Reggie Kray 2. Lizzie Borden 3. The Boston Strangler 4. Alcatraz 5. Myra Hindley 6. Bonnie and Clyde 7. Brinks Mat 8. Charles Manson 9. Charles Lindbergh 10. Legs Diamond

QUIZ 42

. . . .

1 A bronze statue of Billy Bremner stands outside which football club's ground?

2 Which city is served by Frederic Chopin Airport?

3 Who created the private eye Philip Marlowe?

4 What was Margaret Thatcher's maiden name?

5 Which cartoon villain vies with Popeye for the attentions of Olive Oyl?

6 Pinkie Brown is the name of a sadistic gangster in which novel and film?

7 Which colonel was played by Laurence Harvey in the film *The Alamo*?

8 In what year did Martina Navratilova win her first Wimbledon Singles title?

9 Which former butler of Princess Diana was cleared of theft in 2002?

10 Tony Hadley provided lead vocals for which chart-topping band of the 1980s?

ANSWERS

1. Leeds United 2. Warsaw 3. Raymond Chandler 4. Roberts 5. Bluto
6. *Brighton Rock* 7. Colonel Travis 8. 1978 9. Paul Burrell 10. Spandau Ballet

QUIZ 43

• •

1 Who played Mrs King in *The Scarecrow And Mrs King*?

2 How many people called Baker have played Dr Who?

3 Who played the role of George Carter in *The Sweeney*?

4 In which cult series did Agent Dale Cooper attempt to solve the murder of Laura Palmer?

5 In *Star Trek: The Next Generation*, who plays the role of Guinan?

6 In which *Star Trek* spin-off did Captain Kathryn Janeway assume command?

7 Who did Robert Stack play in the TV series *The Untouchables*?

8 Which gang is led by a gangster called Clyde in *Wacky Races*?

9 In *Starsky and Hutch* what is the first name of Starsky?

10 In *Starsky and Hutch* what is the first name of Hutch?

ANSWERS

1. Kate Jackson 2. Two, Tom and Colin 3. Dennis Waterman 4. *Twin Peaks*
5. Whoopi Goldberg 6. *Star Trek: Voyager* 7. Elliot Ness 8. The Ant Hill Mob
9. Dave 10. Ken

QUIZ 44

. . . .

1   What is the name of Homer Simpson's only son?

2   What is the name of Victor Meldrew's long-suffering wife?

3   In which series did PC Bradley replace PC Rowan?

4   What is the name of Tony Soprano's wife in *The Sopranos*?

5   In the comedy series *Frasier*, what is Frasier's medical speciality?

6   In which western series did Clint Eastwood play Rowdy Yates?

7   In which US state does Magnum PI carry out his investigations?

8   Who played the role of Cain in the TV series *Kung Fu*?

9   In which series did Ted Danson play Sam Malone?

10 Who played the title role in *A Man Called Ironside*?

ANSWERS

1. Bart 2. Margaret 3. *Heartbeat* 4. Carmela 5. Psychiatry 6. *Rawhide*
7. Hawaii 8. David Carradine 9. *Cheers* 10. Raymond Burr

QUIZ 45

• •

What are the first names of the following real life and
fictional characters?

1 Inspector Clouseau

2 Hotlips Houlihan

3 Madame Tussaud

4 Lucky Luciano

5 The Elephant Man

6 CS Lewis

7 Kid Curry

8 DH Lawrence

9 Inspector Kojak

10 Dr Crippen

ANSWERS

1. Jacques 2. Margaret 3. Marie 4. Charles 5. John 6. Clive Staples 7. Jed
8. David Herbert 9. Theo 10. Harvey

QUIZ 46

• •

1 What is the transport link between John F Kennedy, Marco Polo and John Lennon?

2 Who was the first English king to be killed by an arrow?

3 Which jazz singer was known as Lady Day?

4 Which Z is the name of the father of the Apostles James and John?

5 Who recorded the albums *The Piano Man* and *An Innocent Man*?

6 By what name is John Reid better known when donning a black mask?

7 Who played a villain in the film *The Road To Perdition* and a hero in the film *The Sting*?

8 Who was appointed Archbishop of Canterbury in 2002?

9 Which foe of Batman was played on TV by George Sanders and on film by Arnold Schwarzenegger?

10 Which Charlie Chaplin film was a parody on Adolf Hitler?

ANSWERS

1. All have airports named after them 2. Harold II 3. Billie Holliday
4. Zebadee 5. Billy Joel 6. The Lone Ranger 7. Paul Newman 8. Rowan
Williams 9. Mr Freeze 10. *The Great Dictator*

QUIZ 47

• •

Which Shakespeare play features the following villains?

1 Shylock

2 Octavia

3 Goneril

4 Iago

5 Sir Piers Exton

6 King Alonso

7 Duke Frederick

8 Polonius

9 The three witches

10 Don John

ANSWERS

1. *The Merchant Of Venice* 2. *Antony and Cleopatra* 3. *King Lear* 4. *Othello*
5. *Richard II* 6. *The Tempest* 7. *As You Like It* 8. *Hamlet* 9. *Macbeth*
10. *Much Ado About Nothing*

QUIZ 48

• •

1 In 1962, who became the first American astronaut to orbit the Earth?

2 Who led the victorious troops at the Battle of Issus in 333BC?

3 Which queen's reputed last words were "All my possessions for a moment of time"?

4 Which 19th-century hero commanded the 7th Battalion of the 7th Cavalry?

5 Which woman won the Nobel Peace Prize in 1979?

6 What is the presidential connection between the years 1865, 1881, 1901 and 1963?

7 Which political party did Anthony Eden represent?

8 Who was the first person to be buried at Poets' Corner?

9 Was Leon Trotsky killed with a dagger, an icepick or a revolver?

10 Who made his final diary entry on May 31, 1669

ANSWERS

1. John Glenn 2. Alexander the Great 3. Queen Elizabeth I 4. General George Custer 5. Mother Teresa 6. Assassinations of US presidents 7. Conservative 8. Geoffrey Chaucer 9. Icepick 10. Samuel Pepys

QUIZ 49

• •

1 Who played the role of Annie Porter in the films *Speed* and *Speed 2*?

2 Who played the villain in the film *Wild Wild West* and the hero in *Dead Again*?

3 What is the character name of the Beverly Hills Cop as played by Eddie Murphy?

4 Which building did King Kong carry Fay Wray to the top of?

5 Who played the leader of the Mexican outlaws in *The Magnificent Seven*?

6 Which detective went in search of the Maltese Falcon?

7 Which film co-starring Daniel Day Lewis and Emma Thompson told the story of the Guildford Four?

8 Which nightmarish villain has been played in a series of films by Robert Englund?

9 Who played the title role in the 1969 musical *Oliver*?

10 Which film earned Louise Fletcher an Oscar for her portrayal of a malicious nurse called Mildred Ratched?

ANSWERS

1. Sandra Bullock 2. Kenneth Branagh 3. Axel Foley 4. Empire State Building
5. Eli Wallach 6. Sam Spade 7. *In The Name Of The Father* 8. Freddy Krueger
9. Mark Lester 10. *One Flew Over The Cuckoo's Nest*

QUIZ 50

• •

1   Which film directed by Mel Gibson tells the story of William Wallace?

2   Which film hero left his home in Walkabout Creek for a series of adventures in New York?

3   Who played the role of Elliott in *E.T.*?

4   What is the name of the central family in the *Godfather* trilogy?

5   Which son of Bruce Lee followed his father into the acting business?

6   What is the first name of the character played by Macauley Culkin in *Home Alone*?

7   Who won an Oscar for his role of an American footballer called Rod Tidwell in *Jerry Maguire*?

8   Which actor swept Debra Winger off her feet at the end of the film *An Officer And A Gentleman*?

9   In which film did James Dean play the role of Caleb Trask?

10 In how many films did Mel Gibson star as Mad Max?

ANSWERS

1. *Braveheart* 2. *Crocodile Dundee* 3. Henry Thomas 4. Corleone
5. Brandon Lee 6. Kevin 7. Cuba Gooding Jnr 8. Richard Gere 9. *East Of Eden* 10. Four (the fourth released in 2004)

QUIZ 51

• •

1 What did Captain Thomas Blood attempt to steal in 1671?

2 Who was found guilty of the A6 murder in 1961?

3 In which film did Phil Collins play one of the Great Train Robbers?

4 Who was convicted of the murder of the 1960s gangster George Cornwell?

5 Which jockey received a prison sentence in 1987 for tax evasion?

6 Whose crimes were recounted in the film *Rogue Trader*?

7 In 1982 which sports car manufacturer was arrested on drug smuggling charges?

8 Which art advisor for the Queen was exposed as a spy in 1979?

9 Who was beheaded for treason at Fotheringay Castle in 1587?

10 Which famed work of art was stolen from the Louvre in 1911 by Vicenzo Perrugia?

ANSWERS

1. The Crown Jewels 2. James Hanratty 3. Buster 4. Ronnie Kray 5. Lester Piggott 6. Nick Leeson 7. John De Lorean 8. Anthony Blunt 9. Mary Queen of Scots 10. *Mona Lisa*

QUIZ 52

1 In the Bible who is the younger brother of Cain and Abel?

2 Which duo wrote the song 'You'll Never Walk Alone'?

3 What is the meteorological nickname of the snooker hero Jimmy White?

4 Whom did David Essex play in the stage musical *Godspell*?

5 Who became Princess Royal in 1987?

6 Which long-serving director of the FBI died in 1972?

7 In the early days of which sport did Gentleman Jim Corbett face Bob Fitzsimmons?

8 Which Welsh born singer was 'Holding Out For A Hero' in 1985?

9 Which children's comic featured the character of Beryl the Peril?

10 By what four-letter name is the rock star born Paul Hewson better known?

ANSWERS

1. Seth 2. Rodgers and Hammerstein 3. Whirlwind 4. Jesus 5. Princess Anne 6. J Edgar Hoover 7. Boxing 8. Bonnie Tyler 9. Dandy 10. Bono (of U2)

QUIZ 53

• •

1. Who played a guardian angel called Jonathan Smith in *Highway To Heaven*?

2. Who replaced Farrah Fawcett as a Charlie's Angel?

3. Which seaside resort houses Basil Fawlty's hotel, Fawlty Towers?

4. Which animated crime fighter is assisted by a cat called Spot?

5. Sarek is the father of which *Star Trek* character?

6. Which comedy double act portrayed the characters of Charlie Farley and Piggy Malone?

7. Which loyal servant is played by Tony Robinson in *Blackadder*?

8. What is Captain Mainwaring's daytime job in *Dad's Army*?

9. Cindy Bear is the girlfriend of which cartoon hero?

10. Which pink aliens lived on a blue moon with the Soup Dragon and the Froglets?

ANSWERS

1. Michael Landon 2. Cheryl Ladd 3. Torquay 4. Hong Kong Phooey 5. Mr Spock 6. The Two Ronnies 7. Baldrick 8. Bank manager 9. Yogi Bear 10. The Clangers

QUIZ 54

• •

1   What is the name of Fred Flintstone's wife?

2   What is the name of Fred Flintstone's pet dinosaur?

3   Which medal was Inspector Jack Frost awarded, after being shot in the head on duty?

4   Who played the role of George Cowley in *The Professionals*?

5   Which series featured the cop partners of Bobby Hill and Andy Renko?

6   What is the first name of the Fonz?

7   What is the name of the female counterpart of He Man?

8   Which family is served by a butler called Lurch?

9   Who played Starsky in the TV series *Starsky and Hutch*?

10 What is the first name of the TV detective Cannon played by William Conrad?

ANSWERS

1. Wilma 2. Dino 3. George Cross 4. Gordon Jackson 5. *Hill Street Blues*
6. Arthur 7. She-Ra 8. The Addams Family 9. Paul Michael Glaser 10. Frank

QUIZ 55

1 Which wild west heroine has been played on film by Doris Day, Jane Russell and Ellen Barkin?

2 In which town was Wyatt Earp involved in the Gunfight At The OK Corral?

3 What is the four-letter surname of Buffalo Bill?

4 In which western movie classic did John Wayne play the Ringo Kid?

5 What was the home state of Davy Crockett?

6 Which wild west hero rode a horse called Diablo?

7 Butch Cassidy, Kid Curry and The Sundance Kid were all members of which gang?

8 Red Connors was the sidekick of which fictional wild west hero?

9 In which film did Clint Eastwood first play 'The Man With No Name'?

10 Who played the title role in the TV western *The Virginian*?

ANSWERS

1. Calamity Jane 2. Tombstone 3. Cody 4. *Stagecoach* 5. Tennessee 6. The Cisco Kid 7. The Hole In The Wall Gang 8. Hopalong Cassidy 9. *A Fistful Of Dollars* 10. James Drury

QUIZ 56

• •

1 Who created the aristocratic sleuth Lord Peter Wimsey?

2 What six-letter surname connects the composer Scott and the singer Janis?

3 Who created the character of Bertie Wooster?

4 What is the name of Orville Wright's brother?

5 Who was the first American woman in space?

6 After whom were Teddy Bears named?

7 Who wrote the book *Mein Kampf*?

8 Which opera features a highwayman called MacHeath?

9 What type of animal was Little John in Disney's animated version of *Robin Hood*?

10 By what five-letter name is Gordon Sumner better known?

ANSWERS

1. Dorothy L Sayers 2. Joplin 3. PG Wodehouse 4. Wilbur 5. Sally Ride
6. Theodore Roosevelt 7. Adolf Hitler 8. *The Beggar's Opera* 9. Bear
10. Sting

QUIZ 57

• •

Who created the following literary heroes?

1 Richard Hannay

2 John Ridd

3 Jim Hawkins

4 Brigadier Gerard

5 Bilbo Baggins

6 Poldark

7 Porthos

8 Frederick Trotteville

9 Ivanhoe

10 The Scarlet Pimpernel

ANSWERS

1. John Buchan 2. RD Blackmore 3. Robert Louis Stevenson 4. Arthur Conan Doyle 5. JRR Tolkein 6. Winston Graham 7. Alexandre Dumas 8. Enid Blyton 9. Sir Walter Scott 10. Baroness Orczy

QUIZ 58

. . . .

1 Which British monarch was beheaded in 1649?

2 Which 19th-century Italian revolutionary's followers were known as the Red Shirts?

3 Who is known as the Father Of Television?

4 Which president of the USA authorized the dropping of the first atom bomb in World War II?

5 Which dictator was shot in the nose by Violet Gibson in 1936?

6 In which century was Martin Luther excommunicated by the Roman Catholic church?

7 Who designed the steam ship *The Great Eastern*?

8 In which century was the furniture maker Thomas Chippendale born?

9 Which king of Phrygia had a golden touch?

10 Which Soviet leader died in 1984?

ANSWERS

1. Charles I 2. Garibaldi 3. John Logie Baird 4. Harry S Truman 5. Benito Mussolini 6. 16th century 7. Isambard Kingdom Brunel 8. 18th century 9. King Midas 10. Yuri Andropov

QUIZ 59

• •

1 In which 1962 film did Elvis Presley play a boxer?

2 What was the title of the third film in which Anthony Hopkins played Hannibal Lecter?

3 In which film did Robert De Niro play a psychopath called Max Cady?

4 In which 1994 film did Bruce Willis shoot dead John Travolta?

5 In which film did Daniel Day Lewis suffer from cerebral palsy?

6 Who played one third of the Witches Of Eastwick and one half of Thelma And Louise?

7 In which war epic did Tom Hanks play Captain John Miller?

8 In a 1995 film, which Scottish hero was portrayed by Liam Neeson?

9 What is the name of the superhero played by Dom Deluise in *The Cannonball Run*?

10 Who played Che Guevara in the 1996 film *Evita*?

ANSWERS

1. *Kid Galahad* 2. *Red Dragon* 3. *Cape Fear* 4. *Pulp Fiction* 5. *My Left Foot*
6. Susan Sarandon 7. *Saving Private Ryan* 8. Rob Roy 9. Captain Chaos
10. Antonio Banderas

QUIZ 60

. . . .

1 Which member of the Marx Brothers was christened Leonard?

2 Who directed the Oscar winning epic *Gandhi*?

3 Who played a hero in the films *The Rookie*, *Platoon* and *Navy Seals*?

4 In which film did Tom Cruise and Nicole Kidman play a married couple called Bill and Alice Harford?

5 In which black and white 1960s movie did Richard Harris play a rugby league hero called Frank Machin?

6 Which film star born in Lancashire was nicknamed Sexy Rexy?

7 Who played the assassin in the 1973 film *The Day Of The Jackal*?

8 Who directed the spaghetti western *The Good, The Bad And The Ugly*?

9 Which movie icon was nicknamed The Little Tramp?

10 Who did Emilio Estevez play in the film *Young Guns*?

ANSWERS

1. Chico 2. Richard Attenborough 3. Charlie Sheen 4. *Eyes Wide Shut*
5. *This Sporting Life* 6. Rex Harrison 7. Edward Fox 8. Sergio Leone
9. Charlie Chaplin 10. Billy the Kid

QUIZ 61

. . . .

Unravel the anagrams to give the names of ten
   criminals.

1 NEAR IN YORK

2 THY BASIC SCUD

3 A LEAN COP

4 LEND KYLE

5 GAWKY FUSE

6 LIBEL KISS

7 BACK JURY

8 CLANSMAN HORSE

9 LACK BED BAR

10 SINGING BORE

ANSWERS

1. Ronnie Kray 2. Butch Cassidy 3. Al Capone 4. Ned Kelly 5. Guy Fawkes
6. Bill Sikes 7. Jack Ruby 8. Charles Manson 9. Blackbeard 10. Ronnie Biggs

QUIZ 62

. . . .

1 Which explorer wrote the book *Everest The Hard Way*?

2 Who captained the *Bounty*, taken over by a mutinous crew?

3 After which god was Wednesday named?

4 Which teacher portrayed on film by Maggie Smith taught at the Marcia Blaine School for Girls?

5 Which Irish musician became known as The Man With The Golden Flute?

6 Which former British prime minister had the middle name of Ewart?

7 In which decade was John Lennon born?

8 Who was the first Plantaganet king of England?

9 On TV, who was the sheriff of Four Feather Falls?

10 Which blues legend named his guitar Lucille?

ANSWERS

1. Chris Bonnington 2. Captain Bligh 3. Woden 4. Miss Jean Brodie
5. James Galway 6. William Gladstone 7. 1940s 8. Henry II 9. Tex Tucker
10. BB King

QUIZ 63

• •

1 Skaro is the home planet of which robotic villains?

2 Which Mississippi lawman was continually at loggerheads with Musky Muskrat?

3 In *Star Trek*, what is the colour of Mr Spock's blood?

4 Who played BA Baracus in *The A Team*?

5 Who links the TV shows *Monty Python*, *Ripping Yarns* and *Pole To Pole*?

6 In which prison was Norman Stanley Fletcher incarcerated in *Porridge*?

7 Who plays Dalziel in *Dalziel And Pascoe*?

8 Captain Scarlet worked for which organization?

9 Who piloted *Thunderbird 2*?

10 Who plays the role of Tony Soprano in *The Sopranos*?

ANSWERS

1. The Daleks 2. Deputy Dawg 3. Green 4. Mr T 5. Michael Palin 6. Slade
7. Warren Clarke 8. Spectrum 9. Virgil Tracy 10. James Gandolfini

QUIZ 64

• •

1. Who played Winston Churchill in *The Wilderness Years*?

2. Which actor penned an autobiography entitled *I Am The Doctor*?

3. Who plays the role of Dana Scully in *The X Files*?

4. Which cartoon cat was the adversary of Pixie and Dixie?

5. In which series did Leonard Nimoy play the role of Paris?

6. In which city did David Addison and Maddie Hayes carry out their investigations in *Moonlighting*?

7. Who played Jeannie in *I Dream Of Jeannie*?

8. Which actor has appeared in more episodes of *The Avengers* than anyone else?

9. Which creator of *The Muppets* died in 1990?

10. Which role was played by Nichelle Nichols in *Star Trek*?

ANSWERS

1. Robert Hardy 2. Jon Pertwee 3. Gillian Anderson 4. Mr Jinks 5. *Mission Impossible* 6. Los Angeles 7. Barbara Eden 8. Patrick Macnee 9. Jim Henson 10. Lieutenant Uhura

QUIZ 65

. . . .

Who recorded the following pop hits in the given
   years?

1   1990 'Just Like Jesse James'
2   1978 'Rasputin'
3   1967 'The Ballad Of Bonnie And Clyde'
4   1972 'Samson And Delilah'
5   1998 'Mulder And Scully'
6   1977 'I Remember Elvis Presley'
7   1981 'Joan Of Arc'
8   1984 'I Feel Like Buddy Holly'
9   1987 'When Smokey Sings'
10 1981 'Bette Davis Eyes'

ANSWERS

1. Cher 2. Boney M 3. Georgie Fame 4. Middle Of The Road 5. Catatonia
6. Danny Mirror 7. OMD 8. Alvin Stardust 9. ABC 10. Kim Carnes

QUIZ 66

. . . .

1 Which frontman for the pop group Pulp was arrested at the 1996 Brit Awards?

2 Which British boxer was nicknamed the Dark Destroyer?

3 What is the job of the computer hero Super Mario?

4 What is Elton John's real first name?

5 What is the first name of Baron Frankenstein?

6 Which terrorist organization was responsible for the deaths of 11 athletes at the 1972 Olympics?

7 Which entertainer was born Michael Dumble Smith?

8 Action Man is the British counterpart of which American doll?

9 Which athlete penned an autobiography entitled *The First Four Minutes*?

10 Which fizzy drink was Dr John Pemberton famed for inventing in 1886?

ANSWERS

1. Jarvis Cocker 2. Nigel Benn 3. Plumber 4. Reginald 5. Victor 6. Black September 7. Michael Crawford 8. GI Joe 9. Roger Bannister 10. Coca Cola

QUIZ 67

• •

1   Which fantasy novel by Michael Ende features a teenage hero called Bastion?

2   Cardinal Richelieu is the sworn enemy of which swashbuckling trio?

3   Which series of novels features a gang of youngsters called The Outlaws?

4   Which author created the character of Dracula?

5   What is the name of the murderer in *The Adventures Of Tom Sawyer*?

6   In which book did the character of George Smiley make his literary debut?

7   Under what name did Alfred Wight write several vet novels?

8   In which mythical land do JM Barrie's *Lost Boys* live?

9   What is Romeo's last name in the Shakespeare play?

10 What is Ali Baba's profession?

ANSWERS

1. *The Never Ending Story* 2. *The Three Musketeers* 3. *Just William* 4. Bram Stoker 5. Injun Joe 6. *The Spy Who Came In From The Cold* 7. James Herriot 8. Never Never Land 9. Montague 10. Woodcutter

QUIZ 68

• •

1 What is the last name of Bonnie Prince Charlie?

2 Who invented the Spinning Jenny?

3 How did TE Lawrence die?

4 Who sailed to Antarctica in a vessel called the *Fram*?

5 For what crime was Anne Boleyn executed?

6 Which E word is the collective name given to the writers of the four Gospels?

7 Who designed the flag of Italy?

8 Who founded the Boy Scout movement?

9 On which island did Nelson Mandela serve a 27-year jail sentence?

10 Who led the victorious English troops at the Battle of Agincourt?

ANSWERS

1. Stuart 2. James Hargreaves 3. In a motorcycle accident 4. Roald Amundsen 5. Adultery 6. Evangelists 7. Napoleon Bonaparte 8. Lord Baden-Powell 9. Robben Island 10. Henry V

QUIZ 69

• •

1 Who played a villain called Grissom in the 1989 film *Batman*?

2 What is the title of the second film in which Paul Newman plays Eddie Felson?

3 Which rodent film hero was created by EB White and voiced by Michael J Fox?

4 Which film starring Sylvester Stallone was set in the year 2032?

5 Who played a convict called Red in *The Shawshank Redemption*?

6 What is the name of the King of the Swingers in *The Jungle Book*?

7 What unusual occurrence links the John Wayne films of *The Alamo*, *The Cowboys* and *The Shootist*?

8 Who connects the films *Bird On A Wire*, *Conspiracy Theory* and *Signs*?

9 In which 1993 film did Bette Midler play an evil witch called Winnie Sanderson?

10 In which Batman movie did Jim Carrey play The Riddler?

ANSWERS

1. Jack Palance 2. *The Color Of Money* 3. Stuart Little 4. *Demolition Man*
5. Morgan Freeman 6. King Louie 7. John Wayne dies in all three films
8. Mel Gibson 9. *Hocus Pocus* 10. *Batman Forever*

QUIZ 70

. . . .

1   Which film marked the big screen debut of Indiana Jones?

2   Who plays Wayne in *Wayne's World*?

3   Which doctor was played by Ben Kingsley in the film *Without A Clue*?

4   Which wife of Clark Gable died in a plane crash?

5   Which movie icon was killed in 1955 driving a Porsche Spyder?

6   Who played the hero in the film *The Pelican Brief* and the villain in *Training Day*?

7   Which Arthurian hero was portrayed by Richard Gere in the film *First Knight*?

8   In which film did Burt Lancaster play Sergeant Warden?

9   Who played Dracula in the 1992 film *Bram Stoker's Dracula*?

10 Which fillm set in Ancient Rome earned an Oscar for Russell Crowe?

ANSWERS

1. *Raiders Of The Lost Ark* 2. Mike Myers 3. Dr Watson 4. Carole Lombard
5. James Dean 6. Denzel Washington 7. Sir Lancelot 8. *From Here To Eternity*
9. Gary Oldman 10. *Gladiator*

QUIZ 71

1 Was the serial killer Peter Kurten nicknamed The Vampire of Danzig, Dusseldorf or Dresden?

2 Which of Hitler's henchmen was known as The Butcher of Lyons?

3 Who was the leader of The People's Temple, a religious cult that committed mass suicide in 1978?

4 Which pirate was appointed Lieutenant-Governor of Jamaica in 1674?

5 What is Al short for in the name of Al Capone?

6 Which film is based on the prison memoirs of Billy Hayes?

7 Who was born first, Ronnie Kray or Reggie Kray?

8 On which island did the Mafia originate?

9 In which South American country did Ronnie Biggs live in exile?

10 By what nickname was the gangster Benjamin Siegel otherwise known?

ANSWERS

1. Dusseldorf 2. Klaus Barbie 3. Reverend Jim Jones 4. Henry Morgan
5. Alphonse 6. *Midnight Express* 7. Ronnie, by 45 minutes 8. Sicily 9. Brazil
10. Bugsy Siegel

QUIZ 72

1 Which animal swallowed Jonah in the Bible?

2 Which film star sang 'Happy Birthday To You' to John F Kennedy in 1962?

3 Which masked hero has a name that is derived from the Spanish word for fox?

4 Which Russian despot died in March 1584, as he was preparing to play a game of chess?

5 Which 20th-century military leader was known as The Desert Fox?

6 Give any year in which Idi Amin was president of Uganda.

7 Who was the head of Hitler's SS?

8 Who was the youngest member of The Beatles?

9 What number of basketball shirt is most associated with Michael Jordan?

10 Which 38-year-old boxing world champion announced his retirement in 2004?

ANSWERS

1. Whale 2. Marilyn Monroe 3. Zorro 4. Ivan the Terrible 5. Erwin Rommel
6. 1971 to 1979 7. Heinrich Himmler 8. George Harrison 9. 23 10. Lennox
Lewis

QUIZ 73

• •

1 Which underwater vessel is commanded by Troy Tempest?

2 In which cartoon series does Isaac Hayes voice the character of Chef?

3 Who played Hutch in the TV series *Starsky and Hutch*?

4 Which outlaw was played by Clive Mantle in *Robin of Sherwood*?

5 What is the name of the clown, the hero of Bart Simpson?

6 Which actor has played the Singing Detective on TV and the headmaster of Hogwarts on film?

7 What is the first name of Rockford in *The Rockford Files*?

8 Pepper Anderson is the lead character in which TV series?

9 In which series did David Jason play the role of Skullion?

10 The TV series *Angel* was a spin-off from which show?

ANSWERS

1. *Stingray* 2. *South Park* 3. David Soul 4. Little John 5. Krusty 6. Michael Gambon 7. Jim 8. *Police Woman* 9. *Porterhouse Blue* 10. *Buffy The Vampire Slayer*

QUIZ 74

. . . .

Unravel the anagrams to give the names of ten TV
   heroes.

1 TORCH WOOD

2 MUD FLEXOR

3 SERMON PRAY

4 TEN SAVE SUIT

5 RECOMPRESS INTO

6 SIN DAMPER

7 COOL BUM

8 HOT JOKER

9 BEG RACER

10 RECORK BUGS

ANSWERS

1. Doctor Who 2. Fox Mulder 3. Perry Mason 4. Steve Austin 5. Inspector
Morse 6. Spiderman 7. Columbo 8. TJ Hooker 9. Bergerac 10. Buck Rogers

QUIZ 75

• •

1   In which Bond movie did Woody Allen and Orson Welles play the villains?

2   Which CIA contact of Bond has played by various actors including Jack Lord and David Hedison?

3   By what shorter name is Major Boothroyd better known?

4   What is the family motto of James Bond and also the title of a Bond movie?

5   In which film did Pierce Brosnan as 007 battle against Sean Bean as 006?

6   In how many films did Roger Moore play James Bond?

7   In which Bond movie did Maud Adams play the title role?

8   In which country was *You Only Live Twice* mainly set?

9   In which film did Roger Moore share passionate scenes with Barbara Bach?

10   In which film did 007 kill Dr Kananga?

ANSWERS

1. *Casino Royale* 2. Felix Leiter 3. Q 4. *The World Is Not Enough*
5. *Goldeneye* 6. Seven 7. *Octopussy* 8. Japan 9. *The Spy Who Loved Me*
10. *Live And Let Die*

QUIZ 76

● ●

1. In what month is St Luke's Day celebrated?

2. Which singer was born Sandra Goodrich?

3. In 1989, Prince Philip controversially attended the funeral of which Asian emperor?

4. What is the nationality of Formula 1 hero Nelson Piquet?

5. Which rock star recorded a greatest hits collection entitled *Hits Out Of Hell*?

6. Which gold-medal-winning athlete of the 1920s was nicknamed The Flying Scotsman?

7. At the start of the 21st century who was minister for the Civil Service in Great Britain?

8. Who created the equine hero of *Black Beauty*?

9. Who is the subject of the hit record 'Geno', by Dexy's Midnight Runners?

10. By what name is Ariel known in the title of a Disney animation?

ANSWERS

1. October 2. Sandie Shaw 3. Emperor Hirohito 4. Brazilian 5. Meat Loaf
6. Eric Liddel 7. Tony Blair 8. Anna Sewell 9. Geno Washington 10. The Little Mermaid

QUIZ 77

• •

1　Who led a gang of pickpockets in Oliver Twist?

2　Which school is attended by Billy Bunter?

3　Ginger and Algy are the best friends of which literary hero?

4　Who created the character of Brother Cadfael?

5　Bathsheba Everdene is the heroine of which classic novel?

6　What is Cinderella's first name in the fairytale?

7　What was Emily Brontë's only novel?

8　Which literary prize, launched in 1969, has been won by Salman Rushdie and Iris Murdoch?

9　In what month is Burn's Night celebrated in Scotland?

10　What is the first name of Tom Sawyer's girlfriend?

ANSWERS

1. Fagin 2. Greyfriars 3. Biggles 4. Ellis Peters 5. *Far From The Madding Crowd*
6. Ella 7. *Wuthering Heights* 8. The Booker Prize 9. January 10 . Becky

QUIZ 78

Unravel the anagrams to give the names of ten
   historical figures

1 CRANKED FAIRS
2 A SLOW CIDER
3 BANNER NOTE
4 GREECES GROUT
5 A WEATHER GRILL
6 CASUAL JURIES
7 A COOL ROMP
8 A FRANCO JOE
9 CHRONIC HULL TWINS
10 LOW MILL COVERER

ANSWERS

1. Francis Drake 2. Oscar Wilde 3. Anne Brontë 4. George Custer 5. Walter
Raleigh 6. Julius Caesar 7. Marco Polo 8. Joan Of Arc 9. Winston Churchill
10. Oliver Cromwell

QUIZ 79

• •

1 Who played the Bandit in the 1977 film *Smokey And The Bandit*?

2 Which lover has been played on film by Richard Chamberlain, Vincent Price and Donald Sutherland?

3 Which film heroes drove a vehicle called The Ectomobile?

4 Who played the villain Bill Sikes in the film musical *Oliver*?

5 Which film saw Harrison Ford searching for his kidnapped wife in Paris?

6 Tom Cruise gained an Oscar nomination for his portrayal of war veteran Ron Kovic in which film?

7 Who played Batgirl in the film *Batman And Robin*?

8 Which ex-husband of Madonna played a convict in *Dead Man Walking*?

9 Which star of the film *The Sixth Sense* was a co-founder of The Planet Hollywood restaurant chain?

10 Which animated film features a pair of villains called Mr and Mrs Tweedy?

ANSWERS

1. Burt Reynolds 2. Casanova 3. *Ghostbusters* 4. Oliver Reed 5. *Frantic*
6. *Born On The Fourth Of July* 7. Alicia Silverstone 8. Sean Penn 9. Bruce
Willis 10. *Chicken Run*

QUIZ 80

• •

1   What was the first name of the character played by Leonardo DiCaprio in *Titanic*?

2   Who wrote the play that inspired the musical *My Fair Lady*?

3   Who played Dr Hammond, the creator of *Jurassic Park*?

4   Which jockey did John Hurt play on film when winning the Grand National on a horse called Aldaniti?

5   Who played Brian in *The Life Of Brian*?

6   Which actor was dirty dancing with Jennifer Grey?

7   Who appeared in the greatest number of Alfred Hitchcock films?

8   Who co-starred with his wife Joanne Woodward in the film *Mr And Mrs Bridges*?

9   Who played the title role in *The Madness Of King George*?

10 Which mean spirited character has been played by Michael Caine, Alastair Sim and Albert Finney?

ANSWERS

1. Jack 2. George Bernard Shaw 3. Richard Attenborough 4. Bob Champion 5. Graham Chapman 6. Patrick Swayze 7. Alfred Hitchcock in cameo roles 8. Paul Newman 9. Nigel Hawthorne 10. Ebenezer Scrooge

QUIZ 81

1 Who committed mass murder in 1987 in the town of Hungerford?

2 A gangster called Rocky Sullivan was the lead character in which Jimmy Cagney movie?

3 How did Anne Bonney gain notoriety in the 18th century?

4 Which criminal first appeared on the big screen in the Hitchcock thriller *The Lodger*?

5 The killer Brenda Spencer provided the inspiration for which 1979 number one hit single?

6 In 1982, Ronald O'Brien became the first man in the USA to be executed by what method?

7 The actor Stacy Keach and the playwright Oscar Wilde were both incarcerated in which prison?

8 In what year was the Yorkshire Ripper arrested?

9 Which politician was portrayed by Ian McKellan in the film *Scandal*?

10 Which rock star played the bank robber John McVicar in a 1980 film?

ANSWERS

1. Michael Ryan 2. *Angels With Dirty Faces* 3. She was a pirate 4. Jack The Ripper 5. 'I Don't Like Mondays' 6. Lethal injection 7. Reading Gaol 8. 1981 9. John Profumo 10. Roger Daltrey

QUIZ 82

. . . .

1 What was the title of The Beatles first chart album?

2 David Bryant was the first world champion in which sport?

3 Which plant did St Patrick use to illustrate the Holy Trinity?

4 Which royal house did Henry VII belong to?

5 Before being elected US president, of which state was Bill Clinton the governor?

6 What is Scooby short for in the name of the canine hero Scooby Doo?

7 Which war hero wrote the book *The Seven Pillars Of Wisdom*?

8 Which award did John Lennon return to Buckingham Palace in protest against the Vietnam War?

9 The ghost of which wife of Henry VIII is said to haunt Hampton Court?

10 In World War II, which British singer was known as The Forces Sweetheart?

ANSWERS

1. *Please Please Me* 2. Bowls 3. Shamrock 4. Tudor 5. Arkansas 6. Scoobert
7. TE Lawrence 8. MBE 9. Catherine Howard 10. Vera Lynn

QUIZ 83

. . . .

1   Who replaced Terry McCann as Arthur Daley's minder?

2   In *NYPD Blue*, which actor played Detective Sorenson?

3   Which TV family live on Mockingbird Lane?

4   Which king was portrayed by Peter Cook in the comedy series *Blackadder*?

5   Who is often seen in the company of a black-and-white cat called Jess?

6   Who played the wife in the TV series *McMillan And Wife*?

7   Which child spy worked for the World Intelligence Network?

8   Who plays the role of Jane Tennison in *Prime Suspect*?

9   Which steam engine is driven by Jones the Steam?

10 What is the name of the snail in *The Magic Roundabout*

ANSWERS

1. Ray Daley 2. Rick Schroeder 3. The Munsters 4. Richard III 5. Postman Pat 6. Susan St James 7. Joe 90 8. Helen Mirren 9. Ivor the Engine 10. Brian

QUIZ 84

. . . .

1   In *Hart To Hart*, what is the name of Jonathan Hart's wife?

2   Who plays the TV role of the detective Maisie Raine?

3   Which American Indian hero was played on TV by Jay Silverheels?

4   Which ranch empire was owned by Big John Cannon?

5   Who played the title roles in the 1960s TV shows *The Prisoner* and *Dangerman*?

6   Which sergeant caused a multitude of problems for Colonel Hall at Fort Baxter?

7   In which US sci-fi series did Ted Shackleford play the heroic Lieutenant Patrick Brogan?

8   How were the superhuman characters of Sharron Macready, Richard Barrett and Craig Stirling known?

9   Who works alongside a female assistant called Wendy and a cement mixer called Dizzy?

10 Who plays the gentle giant Bomber in *Auf Wiedersehen Pet*?

ANSWERS

1. Jennifer 2. Pauline Quirke 3. Tonto 4. The High Chaparral 5. Patrick McGoohan 6. Sergeant Bilko 7. *Space Precinct* 8. The Champions 9. Bob the Builder 10. Pat Roach

QUIZ 85

1 Who played the upper-class villain Gustav Graves in *Die Another Day*?

2 Telly Savalas, Charles Gray and Donald Pleasence have all played which Bond villain?

3 Which film featured a diminuitive villain called Nick Nack?

4 In which Bond movie did Christopher Walken play Max Zorin?

5 Who played the psychotic villain Renard in *The World Is Not Enough*?

6 Which Bond villain has the first name of Auric?

7 Which villain was ejected into outer space by 007 in *Moonraker*?

8 Which metallic-mouthed henchman was portrayed by Richard Kiel in two Bond movies?

9 Which Bond villain possessed three nipples?

10 What item of clothing did the fearsome Oddjob use as a lethal weapon?

ANSWERS

1.Toby Stephens 2.Blofeld 3.*The Man With The Golden Gun* 4.*A View To A Kill* 5.Robert Carlyle 6.*Goldfinger* 7.Hugo Drax 8.Jaws 9.Scaramanga 10. A bowler hat

QUIZ 86

1 Which eye of the Bionic Man is bionic?

2 Which New York detective has been played on film by Richard Roundtree and Samuel L Jackson?

3 Which servant is secretly in love with Cinderella?

4 Who played the role of Bernardo in the movie western *The Magnificent Seven*?

5 Which boxer won a gold medal in Montreal and went on to become world champion at five weights?

6 Who was the first DJ to be heard on Radio 1?

7 At which San Francisco park did The Beatles perform their last public concert?

8 The Marvin Gaye hit 'Abraham, Martin And John' was a tribute to which three men?

9 By what one-word name is the soccer superstar Luiz de Nazario di Lima better known?

10 Which racehorse trainer became known as the Queen of Aintree?

ANSWERS

1. Left eye 2. John Shaft 3. Buttons 4. Charles Bronson 5. Sugar Ray Leonard 6. Tony Blackburn 7. Candlestick Park 8. Abraham Lincoln, JFK and Martin Luther King 9. Ronaldo 10. Jenny Pitman

QUIZ 87

. . . .

1 Which hero from an Aesop fable removed a thorn from a lion's paw?

2 How is Frodo related to Bilbo Baggins?

3 What is the home town of Brother Cadfael?

4 *Not A Penny More, Not A Penny Less* was the first published novel of which author?

5 In which country was Roald Dahl born?

6 Who wrote the novel *Moby Dick*?

7 What is Winnie the Pooh's favourite food?

8 Which nursery rhyme character ventured to sea with silver buckles on his knee?

9 The author Joy Adamson was murdered on which continent?

10 Which US singer/songwriter penned an autobiography entitled *Laughter In The Rain*?

ANSWERS

1. Androcles 2. Nephew and uncle 3. Shrewsbury 4. Jeffrey Archer 5. Wales
6. Herman Melville 7. Honey 8. Bobby Shafto 9. Africa 10. Neil Sedaka

QUIZ 88

1 In which decade did Alexander Fleming discover pennicillin?

2 Which Roman Emperor was killed in AD41?

3 Who became Lord Protector in 1653?

4 What nickname was bestowed upon Vlad Tepes, after his favourite method of execution?

5 In which city did Anne Frank write her famed diary?

6 How many wives did Henry VIII divorce?

7 After which explorer were the Americas named?

8 Who gave his name to sadism?

9 Who circumnavigated the globe in 1519?

10 During which war did Joan of Arc face English troops?

ANSWERS

1. 1920s 2. Caligula 3. Oliver Cromwell 4. Vlad the Impaler 5. Amsterdam
6. Two 7. Amerigo Vespucci 8. Marquis de Sade 9. Ferdinand Magellan
10. One Hundred Years War

QUIZ 89

• •

Unravel the anagrams to give the names of ten film
   stars.

1 A WOOLLY END
2 MASH KNOT
3 INJURED WALES
4 A HOLY DRIVER
5 MICE TOURS
6 BIG MELONS
7 A FILLY SLED
8 CLINK NOTE
9 A DEMONIC LINK
10 SLYER TEMPER

ANSWERS

1. Woody Allen 2. Tom Hanks 3. Julie Andrews 4. Oliver Hardy 5. Tom
Cruise 6. Mel Gibson 7. Sally Field 8. Nick Nolte 9. Nicole Kidman 10. Meryl
Streep •

QUIZ 90

. . . .

1 Who was the first woman to play the role of M in the Bond movies?

2 Which devillish villain has been portrayed by Harvey Stephens, Jonathan Scott-Taylor and Sam Neill?

3 On film how are Alexandra Medford, Jane Spofford and Sukie Ridgemont collectively known?

4 Who played Julius Caesar when Elizabeth Taylor played Cleopatra?

5 What kind of animal is Rafiki in *The Lion King*?

6 In which film did Eddie Murphy play a convict called Reggie Hammond?

7 Which *Star Wars* hero constructed C3P0?

8 What nickname was given to the jewel thief in *The Pink Panther*?

9 In which film did Robert Carlyle shed his clothes in Sheffield?

10 Which actor plays the hapless British spy Johnny English?

ANSWERS

1.Judi Dench 2.Damian Thorn in the *Omen* movies 3.*The Witches Of Eastwick* 4.Rex Harrison 5.A baboon 6.*48 Hours* 7.Anakin Skywalker 8.The Phantom 9.*The Full Monty* 10.Rowan Atkinson

QUIZ 91

. . . .

1 Who escaped from Wormwood Scrubs in 1966 whilst serving a 41-year jail sentence?

2 Which world champion was given the prison number 922335?

3 Who was convicted of the kidnap of estate agent Stephanie Slater?

4 What type of wine did Hannibal Lecter drink to wash down one of his victim's livers?

5 Which number of the Ten Commandments was broken by Jack The Ripper and the Boston Strangler?

6 Which 1994 film directed by Oliver Stone was blamed for copycat crimes in Louisiana?

7 In which city did burglars break into the Watergate building?

8 Which murderous London barber lived on Fleet Street?

9 In 1982, Michael Fagin made news headlines by sitting on whose bed?

10 Who played the outlaw the Sundance Kid in the 1969 film *Butch Cassidy And The Sundance Kid*?

ANSWERS

1. George Blake 2. Mike Tyson 3. Michael Sams 4. Chianti 5. The 6th commandment (Thou shalt not kill) 6. *Natural Born Killers* 7. Washington DC 8. Sweeney Todd 9. Queen Elizabeth II 10. Robert Redford

QUIZ 92

1 In 1991 which Russian leader's statue was removed from Red Square?

2 Which G has been the second most popular name for Popes?

3 What is the last name of Maid Marian, the love of Robin Hood?

4 Which fashion designer's funeral was attended in 1997 by Elton John and Princess Diana?

5 Professor Charles Xavier is the mentor of which group of superheroes?

6 Who resigned as the England rugby union captain in 1996?

7 Who created a public outcry after she tore up a picture of the Pope on live US TV in 1993?

8 What is the name of Batman's butler?

9 In which city was Martin Luther King assassinated?

10 Who solved the murder on the *Orient Express*?

ANSWERS

1. Lenin 2. Gregory 3. Fitzwalter 4. Gianni Versace 5. X Men 6. Will Carling
7. Sinead O'Connor 8. Alfred 9. Memphis 10. Hercule Poirot

QUIZ 93

. . . .

1 David Brent is the central character of which award-winning comedy series?

2 In 1978 who became ITV's first national female newsreader?

3 Which Stone Age cartoon character is the father of Bam Bam?

4 Who created *Star Trek*?

5 Who played the title role in the 1980s TV series *Buck Rogers In The 25th Century*?

6 In which sitcom does David Jason play a shop assistant called Granville?

7 What does the T stand for in the name of the TV cop TJ Hooker?

8 Bo, Luke, Vance and Daisy are all members of which TV family from Hazzard county?

9 Which TV duo took their orders from Captain Dobie?

10 Who played Lois Lane in *The New Adventures Of Superman*?

ANSWERS

1. *The Office* 2. Anna Ford 3. Barney Rubble 4. Gene Roddenberry 5. Gil Gerard 6. *Open All Hours* 7. Thomas 8. Dukes 9. Starsky and Hutch 10. Teri Hatcher

QUIZ 94

. . . .

1 Which Glaswegian policeman played by Mark McManus was based at Maryhill Station?

2 In which comedy series did Estelle Getty play the role of Sophia Weinstock?

3 On which island do Father Ted, Father Jack and Father Dougal share a home?

4 Which marine creature is the best friend of Sandy Ricks?

5 In a popular TV sitcom what was the surname of the brothers Adrian, Joey and Billy?

6 Who played Kelly Garrett in *Charlie's Angels*?

7 How are Mike, Neil, Viv and Rik collectively known?

8 Who played Howling Mad Murdock in *The A Team*?

9 Which TV duo accompanied a tortoise called Old Slowcoach?

10 Who played the role of Corporal Klinger in the TV series *M.A.S.H.*?

ANSWERS

1. Taggart 2. *The Golden Girls* 3. Craggy Island 4. Flipper 5. Boswell (in *Bread*) 6. Jaclyn Smith 7. *The Young Ones* 8. Dwight Schultz 9. Bill and Ben 10. Jamie Farr

QUIZ 95

• •

1 Which country was ruled by the tyrannical Pol Pot?

2 Who wrote the book *Mussolini:His Part In My Downfall*?

3 By what name was the dictator François Duvalier better known?

4 The Stauffenberg Plot of 1944 was an assassination attempt on whom?

5 Which Russian dictator had a name meaning Man Of Steel?

6 Who seized power from Milton Obote in 1971?

7 Who became leader of Zimbabwe in 1980?

8 In 2001 which Yugoslavian dictator was brought before the International War Crimes Tribunal at the Hague?

9 Which Asian dictator wrote down his thoughts in a little red book?

10 Which South American country fell under the rule of General Pinochet following a military coup?

ANSWERS

1. Cambodia 2. Spike Milligan 3. Papa Doc 4. Adolf Hitler 5. Stalin 6. Idi Amin 7. Robert Mugabe 8. Slobodan Milosevic 9. Chairman Mao 10. Chile

QUIZ 96

• •

1 Who succeeded Jeremy Thorpe as leader of the Liberal Party?

2 Which original member of The Beatles died in Hamburg in 1962?

3 Which member of the royal family founded the charity Children In Crisis?

4 Which rock and roll hero was backed by the Comets?

5 Which French leader officially opened the Channel Tunnel alongside Queen Elizabeth II in 1994?

6 In which country was Ferdinand Porsche born?

7 Which Soviet statesman died in February 1984?

8 Who is the older of the Oasis brothers, Noel or Liam?

9 Who is known as The Vicar of Christ?

10 Which playwright became the third husband of Marilyn Monroe?

ANSWERS

1. David Steele 2. Stuart Sutcliffe 3. Sarah Ferguson 4. Bill Haley 5. François Mitterand 6. Austria 7. Yuri Andropov 8. Noel 9. The Pope 10. Arthur Miller

QUIZ 97

• •

1 What is the last name of the literary heroine Anne of Green Gables?

2 Which Foreign Legion hero was created by PC Wren?

3 Which literary trio had the pseudonyms of Ellis, Acton and Currer Bell?

4 Who is the son of Bungo Baggins and Belladonna Took?

5 Which author did Charles Darwin replace on the back of a £10 note?

6 By what shorter name is the hero James Bigglesworth better known?

7 By what name is the fantasizing character of William Fisher better known?

8 Which Robert Burns hero gave his name to a type of headgear?

9 Which French author penned the novel *Les Misérables*?

10 Who created *The Borrowers*?

ANSWERS

1. Shirley 2. Beau Geste 3. The Brontë sisters 4. Bilbo Baggins 5. Charles Dickens 6. Biggles 7. Billy Liar 8. Tam o' Shanter 9. Victor Hugo 10. Mary Norton

QUIZ 98

• •

1 Who was assassinated while enjoying a play entitled *Our American Cousin*?

2 Which decade witnessed the funeral of the Duke Of Wellington?

3 In 1929, Fred Perry was crowned world champion at which sport?

4 What was the first name of the wild west hero Doc Holliday?

5 Which army was founded by William Booth?

6 Which British prime minister attended the Potsdam Peace Conference in 1945?

7 How many English kings have been called Stephen?

8 In 1978, which knighted actor's body was stolen from his grave?

9 Which prolific inventor was known as The Wizard of Menlo Park?

10 Who was the last English king to die in battle?

ANSWERS

1. Abraham Lincoln 2. 1850s 3. Table tennis 4. John 5. Salvation Army
6. Clement Atlee 7. One 8. Charlie Chaplin 9. Thomas Alva Edison
10. Richard III

QUIZ 99

• •

1 Which CIA agent has been played on film by Ben Affleck, Harrison Ford and Alec Baldwin?

2 Who won a Best Actress Oscar for her role in the film *Monster's Ball*?

3 In which 1993 film did Bill Murray play a sarcastic weatherman called Phil Connors?

4 Which movie hero has been portrayed on film by James Garner, Robert Mitchum and Humphrey Bogart?

5 Who won a Best Director Oscar for the film *Reds*?

6 In which *Star Trek* movie did William Shatner and Patrick Stewart join forces?

7 Which of Hitler's henchmen was eerily portrayed by Gregory Peck in *The Boys From Brazil*?

8 Who played the role of Miranda Hillard in *Mrs Doubtfire*?

9 In which 1980 film did John Gielgud play a butler called Hobson?

10 Which film legend's life story was chronicled in the biography *Hollywood's Dark Prince*?

ANSWERS

1. Jack Ryan 2. Halle Berry 3. *Groundhog Day* 4. Philip Marlowe 5. Warren Beatty 6. *Star Trek: Generations* 7. Josef Mengele 8. Sally Field 9. *Arthur* 10. Walt Disney

QUIZ 100

1 Which character falls in love with Neo in the *Matrix* films?

2 In which 1990 film did Johnny Depp cut Winona Ryder's hair with his metallic hands?

3 In which 1993 film did Clint Eastwood play a presidential bodyguard called Frank Horrigan?

4 In which 1975 film did Richard Dreyfuss play a marine biologist called Hooper?

5 Which character was voiced by Demi Moore in Disney's animated version of *The Hunchback Of Notre Dame*?

6 In which Rocky film did Rocky Balboa face a Russian giant called Ivan Drago?

7 Who bought a controlling share of 20th Century Fox in 1985?

8 Who voiced the character of Buzz Lightyear in *Toy Story*?

9 Who won Best Actress awards at the 2003 Oscars and the 2003 Baftas?

10 Which film director links the films *Beetlejuice*, *Planet Of The Apes* and *Batman*?

ANSWERS

1. Trinity 2. *Edward Scissorhands* 3. *In The Line Of Fire* 4. *Jaws* 5. Esmerelda
6. *Rocky IV* 7. Rupert Murdoch 8. Tim Allen 9. Nicole Kidman 10. Tim
Burton

QUIZ 101

• •

1   Which infamous burglar, sentenced to death in 1878, was known for carrying his tools in a violin case?

2   Which movie star was arrested in 1995 in the company of Divine Brown?

3   Who played Al Capone in the 1987 film *The Untouchables*?

4   Which Scottish pirate was hanged in 1701?

5   Which gangster was born Lester Gillis?

6   In which US state were the Salem witch trials held?

7   Which gang of crooks was led by Alec Guinness in a 1951 film?

8   What name was given to the followers of Charles Manson?

9   Which gang of criminals set up a hideout at Leatherslade Farm?

10 Whose life and subsequent execution was chronicled in the film *Dance With A Stranger*?

ANSWERS

1. Charlie Peace 2. Hugh Grant 3. Robert De Niro 4. Captain Kidd 5. Baby Face Nelson 6. Massachusetts 7. The Lavender Hill Mob 8. The Family 9. The Great Train Robbers 10. Ruth Ellis

QUIZ 102

. . . .

1   What is the first name of Dr Doolittle?

2   Which chess champion was defeated by a computer called Deep Blue in 1997?

3   Who, known for penning the song 'Blue Suede Shoes', died in 1998?

4   Who founded Motown Records?

5   What is the secret identity of Batman's partner Robin?

6   Which ex British prime minister died in 1986?

7   Who is the oldest female tennis star to have won a Grand Slam title?

8   Which year of the 20th century witnessed three popes?

9   In 1999, the Citroen car company named their latest model after which famous painter?

10 From which mountain did Moses deliver the Ten Commandments?

ANSWERS

1. John 2. Gary Kasparov 3. Carl Perkins 4. Berry Gordy Jnr 5. Dick Grayson
6. Harold Macmillan 7. Martina Navratilova 8. 1978 9. Picasso 10. Mount Sinai

QUIZ 103

• •

1 In which TV drama did John Thaw play the author Peter Mayle?

2 Who plays the short-tempered Dr Becker in the US comedy series *Becker*?

3 In which decade did John Logie Baird invent television?

4 Which US series features Neil Patrick Harris playing a boy genius?

5 Which wise-cracking fox was voiced for many years by Ivan Owen?

6 Which accident-prone character was portrayed by Michael Crawford in *Some Mothers Do Ave Em*?

7 In *Friends*, what was Monica's last name before her marriage to Chandler Bing?

8 Which Avenger was played on TV by Diana Rigg and on film by Uma Thurman?

9 What is the surname of the central family in *The Beverly Hillbillies*?

10 What was the surname of the central family in the 1960s TV western *Bonanza*?

ANSWERS

1. *A Year In Provence* 2. Ted Danson 3. 1920s 4. Doogie Howser 5. Basil Brush 6. Frank Spencer 7. Geller 8. Emma Peel 9. Clampett 10. Cartwright

QUIZ 104

. . . .

1 Which star of the US TV series *Burke's Law* was born Eugene Klass?

2 Who killed Bobby Ewing in *Dallas* before he was miraculously resurrected in the Southfork shower?

3 Brigadier Lethbridge Stewart is a character in which long-running TV series?

4 Which genial sergeant was portrayed by John Le Mesurier in *Dad's Army*?

5 Who played the title role in *TJ Hooker*?

6 Which TV series featured a convict called Harry Grout?

7 What is the favourite sporting pastime of Fred Flintstone and Barney Rubble?

8 Which Dutch detective had the first name of Piet?

9 Which piece of classical music was used as the TV theme for the *Lone Ranger*?

10 Who created the character of Dame Edna Everage?

ANSWERS

1. Gene Barry 2. Katherine Wentworth 3. Dr Who 4. Sergeant Wilson
5. William Shatner 6. *Porridge* 7. Ten pin bowling 8. Van Der Valk 9. *William Tell Overture* 10. Barry Humphries

QUIZ 105

• •

1 In what year did Roger Bannister run the first sub-four-minute mile?

2 Which American jockey, who died in 2003, rode over 8800 winners in an illustrious 41 year career?

3 Which goalkeeper won 119 caps for Northern Ireland?

4 Under what name did the grappler Shirley Crabtree become better known?

5 Which Australian sporting hero founded his own sports promotion company called Great White Shark?

6 Who are the only duo to have been voted BBC Sports Personality Of The Year?

7 Which country did goalkeeper Bruce Grobbelar represent at international level?

8 In what year did Virginia Wade win the Wimbledon Singles title?

9 Which tennis hero was immortalized by a Wimbledon statue in 1984?

10 Which motorcycle world champion acquired the nickname of the Lion King?

ANSWERS

1. 1954 2. Willie Shoemaker 3. Pat Jennings 4. Big Daddy 5. Greg Norman
6. Torvill and Dean 7. Zimbabwe 8. 1977 9. Fred Perry 10. Carl Fogarty

QUIZ 106

1 Who killed a nine-headed monster called the Hydra?

2 At the 2002 soccer World Cup, which player won the Golden Boot Award with eight goals?

3 Which boy band comprised Jason, Gary, Howard, Robbie and Mark?

4 Prior to 2000, how many US presidents had the first name of James?

5 By what name is the super-villain Edward Nygma otherwise known?

6 What is the hometown of the comic strip hero Desperate Dan?

7 In which sport is Bruce Penhall a former world champion?

8 In what year was *Superman* star Christopher Reeve paralyzed in a horse riding accident?

9 What is the nationality of the Formula One star Juan Pablo Montoya?

10 What is the name of the Barber of Seville in the Rossini opera?

ANSWERS

1. Hercules 2. Ronaldo 3. Take That 4. Six 5. The Riddler 6. Cactusville
7. Speedway 8. 1995 9. Colombian 10. Figaro

QUIZ 107

• •

1 The George Bernard Shaw creation *Major Barbara* was a member of which army?

2 In *Treasure Island*, who did the pirate Billy Bones receive the black spot from?

3 What is the title of the novel that marks the death of Inspector Morse?

4 Who created the spy Harry Palmer?

5 In which novel did Jean Valjean receive a prison sentence for stealing a loaf of bread?

6 How are Barbara, Jack, George, Pam, Janet, Peter and Colin collectively known?

7 What is the title of the fifth novel in the *Harry Potter* series?

8 What is the nationality of the Brothers Grimm?

9 Who falls in love with Cathy in *Wuthering Heights*?

10 What is Bram short for in the name of the author Bram Stoker?

ANSWERS

1. Salvation Army 2. Blind Pew 3. *The Remorseful Day* 4. Len Deighton
5. *Les Misérables* 6. *The Secret Seven* 7. *Harry Potter And The Order Of The Phoenix* 8. German 9. Heathcliffe 10. Abraham

QUIZ 108

. . . .

1 Which American statesman invented bifocals and the rocking chair?

2 In which Austrian city was Mozart born?

3 Which Irishman founded his first home for homeless boys in 1870?

4 Which car company was founded by William Lyons?

5 Who committed suicide after his mistaken belief that Cleopatra was dead?

6 To which royal house did George III belong?

7 From which branch of the armed forces did Prince Edward resign in 1987?

8 After whom was the 1953 FA Cup final named?

9 Who became known as the Father of English Printing?

10 What was the name of John F Kennedy's first lady?

ANSWERS

1. Benjamin Franklin 2. Salzburg 3. Dr Barnardo 4. Jaguar 5. Mark Antony
6. Hanover 7. Royal Marines 8. Stanley Matthews 9. William Caxton
10. Jackie

QUIZ 109

1 Who played the loveable character of Uncle Buck in a 1989 film?

2 In which 1987 film was Arnold Schwarzenegger a reluctant contestant in a futuristic game show?

3 Who does Lawrence Fishburne play in the *Matrix* film series?

4 Who played Miss Marple in the 1962 film *Murder She Said*?

5 What was the call sign of Kris Kristofferson in *Convoy*?

6 Which 1964 film saw Elvis Presley working at a carnival?

7 In which series of films does Clint Eastwood bear the badge number 2211?

8 In which 2000 film did Harrison Ford play a killer called Dr Norman Spencer?

9 In which cult movie did Peter Fonda play Wyatt and Dennis Hopper play Billy?

10 In which film did Robert Duvall say "I love the smell of napalm in the morning"?

ANSWERS

1. John Candy 2. *The Running Man* 3. Morpheus 4. Margaret Rutherford
5. Rubber Duck 6. *Roustabout* 7. *Dirty Harry* 8. *What Lies Beneath* 9. *Easy Rider* 10. *Apocalypse Now*

QUIZ 110

1 Who played Albus Dumbledore in the first two *Harry Potter* films?

2 Which film hero was afraid, totally alone and three million light years from home?

3 Who played the title role in the movie epic *El Cid*?

4 Which film villain killed Marion Crane?

5 Who was the male co-star of Bob Hope in seven *Road* movies?

6 In which film did Tom Hanks and Meg Ryan fall in love via the Internet?

7 Which Hollywood star played the villain Mumbles opposite Warren Beatty's Dick Tracy?

8 Who played Cruella De Vil in Disney's live action version of *101 Dalmatians*?

9 Which film was advertised with the publicity blurb "There can be only one"?

10 In which Vietnam War film did Matthew Modine play the role of Private Joker?

ANSWERS

1. Richard Harris 2. E.T. 3. Charlton Heston 4. Norman Bates 5. Bing Crosby
6. *You've Got Mail* 7. Dustin Hoffman 8. Glenn Close 9. *Highlander* 10. *Full Metal Jacket*

QUIZ 111

. . . .

1 In the nursery rhyme what was stolen by Tom the piper's son?

2 Who did Agrippina poison with mushrooms in AD54?

3 In which film did Steve McQueen play a convict called Henri Charrière?

4 In which city are criminals incarcerated in Sing Sing Prison?

5 Whose diaries were forged by Konrad Kajau?

6 Who was assassinated by two members of her bodyguard in October 1984?

7 What is the name of the Japanese equivalent of the Mafia?

8 Which leader of the Unification Church was jailed for tax evasion in 1982?

9 Who played the title role in the 2003 film *Ned Kelly*?

10 Which author created the cannibalistic killer Hannibal Lecter?

ANSWERS

1. A pig 2. Emperor Claudius 3. *Papillon* 4. New York 5. Hitler's 6. Indira Gandhi 7. The Yakuza 8. Reverend Moon 9. Heath Ledger 10. Thomas Harris

QUIZ 112

1 Who did Christopher Plummer portray in the film *Waterloo*?

2 Who founded the Miss World competition?

3 In which town was Margaret Thatcher born?

4 Who founded the famed female dance troupe The Bluebell Girls?

5 Which cartoon villain is forever in pursuit of Roadrunner?

6 What colour is Hopalong Cassidy's horse?

7 Who is the arch foe of Peter Pan?

8 What is the nationality of the tennis star Thomas Muster?

9 Which American hero was played on TV by Fess Parker and on film by John Wayne?

10 Which aid to road safety was invented by Percy Shaw in 1933?

ANSWERS

1. The Duke of Wellington 2. Eric Morley 3. Grantham 4. Margaret Kelly
5. Wile E Coyote 6. White 7. Captain Hook 8. Austrian 9. Davy Crockett
10. Catseye

QUIZ 113

• •

1   Who plays the role of Sybil Fawlty in *Fawlty Towers*?

2   In the *Inspector Morse* tales, which character is married to Valerie?

3   Which star of the comedy series *Friends*, played Gale Weathers in the horror movie *Scream*?

4   Which character from the *Just William* stories was played on TV by Bonnie Langford?

5   In which town is Mrs Goggins the post mistress?

6   Gary, Tony, Deborah and Dorothy are the main characters in which comedy series?

7   What connects the character of Worzel Gummidge with the character of Spud in *Bob The Builder*?

8   In *The A Team* which character had a morbid fear of flying?

9   In *Dad's Army*, which character was often referred to by Captain Mainwaring as a stupid boy?

10 Side Show Bob is the sworn enemy of which animated youngster?

ANSWERS

1. Prunella Scales 2. Inspector Lewis 3. Courtney Cox 4. Violet Elizabeth Bott 5. Greendale 6. *Men Behaving Badly* 7. They are both scarecrows 8. BA Baracus 9. Private Pike 10. Bart Simpson

QUIZ 114

. . . .

1   What is the name of Boysie's wife in *Only Fools And Horses*?

2   What is the name of the wife of Herman Munster?

3   Which month of the year provided the first name of *The Girl From U.N.C.L.E.*?

4   When Burt Ward played Robin, who played Batman?

5   Which cartoon hero claimed that he was smarter than the average bear?

6   Which former star of the comedy series *Bread* directed the 1998 film *Sliding Doors*?

7   Who played the father of Harry H Corbett in *Steptoe And Son*?

8   'My Darling Clementine' is the theme song of which cartoon dog?

9   Who played the role of Vince Pinner in *Just Good Friends*?

10 What type of animal is Sawtooth in *Wacky Races*?

ANSWERS

1. Marlene 2. Lily 3. April 4. Adam West 5. Yogi Bear 6. Peter Howitt
7. Wilfred Brambell 8. Huckleberry Hound 9. Paul Nicholas 10. Beaver

QUIZ 115

1 Which British golfer won the British Open in 1985?

2 Which tennis star penned the book *Serious:The Autobiography*?

3 In December 1999, who was voted BBC Sports Personality Of The Century?

4 In which country was the snooker star James Wattana born?

5 Who made a meal out of Evander Holyfield's ear in a 1997 world title fight?

6 In 2002, which footballer became the first 16 year old to score a goal in England's premiership?

7 Who was the first Australian driver to be crowned Formula One World Champion?

8 Which Czech tennis star won the Ladie's Singles at Wimbledon in 1998?

9 In which sport have Rex Williams and Ray Edmonds both been crowned world champion?

10 Which South African golfer became known as The Man In Black?

ANSWERS

1. Sandy Lyle 2.John McEnroe 3. Muhammed Ali 4. Thailand 5. Mike Tyson
6. Wayne Rooney 7. Jack Brabham 8. Jana Novotna 9. Billiards 10. Gary Player

QUIZ 116

• •

1　What does the S stand for in the name Winston S Churchill?

2　In which city does the Wizard of Oz live?

3　Which saint features on the pope's signet ring?

4　Who played the role of Jim Bowie in the 1960 film *The Alamo*?

5　What was Diana Spencer's middle name?

6　Which Italian striker was the leading goal scorer at the 1982 soccer World Cup?

7　Which Australian city was named after the father of the theory of evolution?

8　What breed of dog is Snoopy?

9　Which inventor of the aqualung sailed in a research ship called the *Calypso*?

10　In Arthurian legend who is the father of Sir Galahad?

ANSWERS

1. Spencer　2. Emerald City　3. St Peter　4. Richard Widmark　5. Frances
6. Paulo Rossi　7. Darwin　8. Beagle　9. Jacques Cousteau　10. Sir Lancelot

QUIZ 117

1 In which country was Rudyard Kipling born?

2 What was the destination of Geoffrey Chaucer's pilgrims?

3 Who played the literary spy Harry Palmer in three films?

4 Which author is commemorated by a statue of a white rabbit in the Welsh town of Llandudno?

5 Which of King Lear's three daughters was murdered?

6 Who was Adrian Mole profoundly in love with?

7 Who preceeded Sir John Betjeman as poet laureate?

8 Which novel by JRR Tolkein was subtitled *There And Back Again*?

9 Which Copenhagen statue is a memorial to Hans Christian Andersen?

10 What did Shakespeare refer to as 'the green-eyed monster'?

ANSWERS

1. India 2. Canterbury 3. Michael Caine 4. Lewis Carroll 5. Cordelia
6. Pandora 7. Cecil Day Lewis 8. *The Hobbit* 9. The Little Mermaid
10. Jealousy

QUIZ 118

. . . .

1 Which monarch created the Church of England?

2 Which US president ended the USA's involvement in the Vietnam War?

3 Which Monacan princess died in 1982?

4 In 1903, who founded the Suffragettes?

5 In 73BC who led a gladitorial revolt against Rome?

6 What is the name of the wife of the Greek god Zeus?

7 What was the first bird that Noah released from the ark?

8 Who, born in the French town of Dole in 1852, gave his name to a heat treatment for milk?

9 In which year was Diana Spencer born?

10 Who was prime minister of Great Britain during the Suez Crisis?

ANSWERS

1. Henry VIII 2. Richard Nixon 3. Princess Grace 4. Emiline Pankhurst
5. Spartacus 6. Hera 7. A raven 8. Louis Pasteur 9. 1961 10. Anthony Eden

QUIZ 119

- -

1 Who played the role of Inspector Dreyfuss in the *Pink Panther* movies?

2 Who won an Oscar in 1981, two years after his daughter?

3 In the 1960 film *The Magnificent Seven*, how many of the seven were left alive at the end of the film?

4 Who has played a goddess in *Clash Of The Titans* and a Mother Superior in *Sister Act*?

5 Who was the first black actor to win a Best Actor Oscar?

6 What is the preferred weapon of a Jedi knight?

7 Which seemingly indestructable character commits the murders in the *Friday The 13th* movies?

8 Which British actor links the films *Mona Lisa*, *Who Framed Roger Rabbit* and *The Long Good Friday*?

9 Who played Thomas Crown in the 1968 version of *The Thomas Crown Affair*?

10 Who played Thomas Crown in the 1999 version of *The Thomas Crown Affair*?

ANSWERS

1. Herbert Lom 2. Henry Fonda 3. Three 4. Maggie Smith 5. Sidney Poitier
6. Light sabre 7. Jason 8. Bob Hoskins 9. Steve McQueen 10. Pierce
Brosnan

QUIZ 120

. . . .

1   Who played the role of Starsky in the 2004 film version of *Starsky And Hutch*?

2   Who played the role of Hutch in the 2004 film version of *Starsky And Hutch*?

3   How are Larry, Curly and Moe collectively known?

4   Who played the hero in the films *Fletch*, *Spies Like Us* and *The Three Amigos*?

5   What is Billy Crystal's profession in the film *Analyze This*?

6   Who played the title role in *Annie Hall*?

7   Who did James Caan play in *The Godfather*?

8   Which child star played the role of Gertie in *E.T.*?

9   Who played Hercule Poirot in the 1974 film *Murder On The Orient Express*?

10 Who played Hercule Poirot in the 1978 film *Death On The Nile*?

ANSWERS

1. Ben Stiller 2. Owen Wilson 3. *The Three Stooges* 4. Chevy Chase
5. Psychiatrist 6. Diane Keaton 7. Sonny Corleone 8. Drew Barrymore
9. Albert Finney 10. Peter Ustinov

QUIZ 121

. . . .

Whodunnit? Who killed …

1 Martin Luther King?

2 John Lennon?

3 Lee Harvey Oswald?

4 Robert Kennedy?

5 Abraham Lincoln?

6 Spencer Perceval?

7 Cock Robin?

8 Billy the Kid?

9 Mahatma Gandhi?

10 Jesse James?

ANSWERS

1. James Earl Ray 2. Mark Chapman 3. Jack Ruby 4. Sirhan Sirhan 5. John
Wilkes Booth 6. John Bellingham 7. The Sparrow 8. Sheriff Pat Garrett
9. Nathuram Godse 10. Bob Ford

QUIZ 122

. . . .

1 Which cartoon character's favourite song is 'The Camptown Races'?

2 Who was the first British singer to win the Eurovision Song Contest?

3 In which year did Prince Charles marry Diana Spencer?

4 In the Bible, who lived to the age of 969?

5 Which group had a 1995 hit with the song 'Search For The Hero'?

6 Which US President said "Ask not what your country can do for you, but what you can do for your country"?

7 What is Stevie short for in the name Stevie Wonder?

8 Speedy Gonzales, the world's fastest mouse, hails from which country?

9 Which book of the Bible chronicled the birth of Moses?

10 Which year marked the 100th anniversary of the death of Queen Victoria?

ANSWERS

1. Foghorn Leghorn 2. Sandie Shaw 3. 1981 4. Methuselah 5. M People
6. John F Kennedy 7. Steveland 8. Mexico 9. Exodus 10. 2001

QUIZ 123

• •

1   Who does John Shea play in *The New Adventures Of Superman*?

2   What is the name of the archenemy of the Tracy family in *Thunderbirds*?

3   In *The Dukes Of Hazzard*, what breed of dog is Flash?

4   Who played the role of Steel in *Sapphire and Steel*?

5   What is the name of Derek Trotter's local pub in *Only Fools And Horses*?

6   Which comedy duo lived on Oil Drum Lane with their horse Hercules?

7   Who played Jeeves when Hugh Lawrie played Wooster?

8   Which TV butler was portrayed by Ted Cassidy?

9   Who played Uncle Albert in *Only Fools And Horses*?

10 Which series first screened in 2003, stars Joe Pantoliano as FBI agent Joe Renato?

ANSWERS

1. Lex Luthor 2. The Hood 3. Basset hound 4. David McCallum 5. The Nag's Head 6. *Steptoe and Son* 7. Stephen Fry 8. Lurch, in *The Addams Family* 9. Buster Merryfield 10. *The Handler*

QUIZ 124

....

What is the TV occupation of …

1   Mitch Buchannon in *Baywatch*?

2   Mickey Murphy in *Camberwick Green*?

3   Ross Geller in *Friends*?

4   Ted Bundy in *Married With Children*?

5   Joyce Davenport in *Hill Street Blues*?

6   Tristan Farnon in *All Creatures Great And Small*?

7   Cliff Clavin in *Cheers*?

8   Private Frazer in *Dad's Army*?

9   Heathcliff Huxtable in *The Cosby Show*?

10 Barney McGrew in *Trumpton*?

ANSWERS

1. Lifeguard 2. Baker 3. Palaeontologist 4. Shoe salesman 5. Defence attorney 6. Vet 7. Postman 8. Undertaker 9. Obstetrician 10. Fireman

QUIZ 125

Unravel the anagrams to give the names of ten sporting heroes.

1 GO ROWDIEST
2 JOIN WINK NYLONS
3 RUN FOR BANK
4 EGG OR BEETS
5 WISER CALL
6 HEAR ANN SEW
7 NO SKY TIME
8 GAFFERS FIT
9 FALCON KID
10 AVERTED VERGES

ANSWERS

1. Tiger Woods 2. Jonny Wilkinson 3. Frank Bruno 4. George Best 5. Carl Lewis 6. Shane Warne 7. Mike Tyson 8. Steffi Graf 9. Nick Faldo 10. Steve Redgrave

QUIZ 126

. . . .

1   Which monarch was nicknamed Silly Billy and The Sailor King?

2   Who was the first British driver to be crowned Formula 1 World Champion?

3   Which Nobel Peace Prize winner was buried in Atlanta in 1968?

4   Which England goalkeeper retired from international football in 1990 with 125 caps?

5   What is the name of the wife of George W Bush?

6   How many people preceded Tony Blair as Labour prime minister?

7   Who did Karen Barber and Nicky Slater succeed as British champions?

8   In 1985, at the age of 22, who became the youngest ever World Chess Champion?

9   Which JM Barrie creation was played on film by Dustin Hoffman in 1991?

10 Which West Indian cricket star's autobiography is entitled *Hitting Across The Line*?

ANSWERS

1. William IV 2. Mike Hawthorn 3. Martin Luther King 4. Peter Shilton
5. Laura 6. Four 7. Torvill and Dean 8. Gary Kasparov 9. Captain Hook
10. Viv Richards

QUIZ 127

1 Who created the character of Miss Jean Brodie?

2 Which Raymond Briggs creation has a son called Mold and a wife called Mildew?

3 What is the nationality of Hercule Poirot?

4 What is the name of James Bond's elder brother?

5 Who was the last poet laureate of the 20th century?

6 Simon Legree is the name of the villain in which classic novel?

7 What is the name of the prince in *The Prince And The Pauper*?

8 What type of factory did Charlie Bucket visit in a children's novel?

9 How is Princess Aurora otherwise known?

10 Which two fairytale characters escaped the clutches of a wicked witch by pushing her into an oven?

ANSWERS

1. Muriel Spark 2. Fungus The Bogeyman 3. Belgian 4. Henry 5. Andrew Motion 6. *Uncle Tom's Cabin* 7. Edward 8. Chocolate factory 9. *Sleeping Beauty* 10. Hansel and Gretel

QUIZ 128

. . . .

1. What is the first name of the man who invented Morse Code?

2. Who succeeded the assassinated William McKinley as US president?

3. In which year of the 1960s did country-and-western legend Jim Reeves perish in a plane crash?

4. By which title was William Joyce otherwise known in World War II?

5. Was Napoleon Bonaparte nicknamed The Little General, The Little Emperor or The Little Corporal?

6. In 2002 Rowan Williams became the 105th person to hold which post?

7. Who won the greatest number of Wimbledon Men's Singles titles in the 1960s?

8. Who won a Nobel Prize for Physics in 1903 and a second Nobel Prize for Chemistry eight years later?

9. Who is the only US president to have governed for 12 years?

10. Which monarch did Queen Victoria succeed?

ANSWERS

1. Samuel 2. Theodore Roosevelt 3. 1964 4. Lord Haw Haw 5. The Little Corporal 6. Archbishop of Canterbury 7. Rod Laver 8. Marie Curie 9. Franklin D Roosevelt 10. William IV

QUIZ 129

• •

1 Which blockbuster marked the screen farewell of Oliver Reed?

2 Who plays the role of Rogue in the 2000 film *X Men*?

3 What was the title of the second film in which Harrison Ford played Han Solo?

4 In which country was the movie star Sophia Loren born?

5 Who played the title role in the 1996 film version of Sergeant Bilko?

6 Which king did Peter O'Toole portray in *The Lion In Winter*?

7 Who cemented his status as a movie idol after playing the title role in the film *American Gigolo*?

8 Which British actress received an Oscar for her performance in the film *A Passage To India*?

9 In which 1999 film did Robin Williams play a robot?

10 In which classic movie did Trevor Howard meet Celia Johnson at a train station?

ANSWERS

1. *Gladiator* 2. Anna Paquin 3. *The Empire Strikes Back* 4. Italy 5. Steve Martin
6. Henry II 7. Richard Gere 8. Dame Peggy Ashcroft 9. *Bicentennial Man*
10. *Brief Encounter*

QUIZ 130

• •

1 Who played the mother of Elvis Presley in the film *Blue Hawaii*?

2 In which film did Kevin Costner play the role of Frank Farmer?

3 The film hero Indiana Jones has a morbid fear of which creatures?

4 Which film saw Sandy as a member of the Pink Ladies and Danny as a member of the T Birds?

5 Who won a Best Supporting Actor Oscar for his role in the film *The Fugitive*?

6 In which film did Barbara Streisand sing 'Secondhand Rose'?

7 In which film did the all-action hero Jack Colton first come to the rescue of the writer Joan Wilder?

8 When Claire Danes played Juliet, who played Romeo?

9 In which film did Brad Pitt play an unlicensed boxer called Tyler Durden?

10 In which 1997 film did Tom Cruise play a sports agent?

ANSWERS

1. Angela Lansbury 2. *The Bodyguard* 3. Snakes 4. *Grease* 5. Tommy Lee Jones 6. *Funny Girl* 7. *Romancing The Stone* 8. Leonardo Di Caprio 9. *Fight Club* 10. *Jerry Maguire*

QUIZ 131

• •

Whodunnit? Who killed …

1 Mary Ann Nichols?

2 Gianni Versace?

3 David Blakely?

4 Sharon Tate?

5 Wild Biil Hickok?

6 William McKinley?

7 King Duncan?

8 Jill Dando?

9 President James Garfield?

10 Archduke Franz Ferdinand?

ANSWERS

1. Jack the Ripper 2. Andrew Cumanan 3. Ruth Ellis 4. The Manson family
5. Jack McCall 6. Leon Czolgosz 7. Macbeth 8. Barry George 9. Charles
Guiteau 10. Gavrilo Princip

QUIZ 132

1 Whom did John Lennon marry in 1969?

2 Which cat created by TS Eliot shares its name with a book of the Old Testament?

3 In which country was Cliff Richard born?

4 Which historical figure, who features on the back of a £5 note, is known as The Mother Of Prison Reform?

5 Which female singer receives backing vocals from The Pips?

6 In the Bible, who performed the dance of the seven veils?

7 In which country did the cartoon hero Tin Tin originate?

8 Which rock and roller had hits singing about Sally, Lucille, Molly and Jenny?

9 In 1989, who became the first English golfer to win the US Masters?

10 Which former first lady of the USA gave her name to a treatment clinic for addictions?

ANSWERS

1. Yoko Ono 2. Deuteronomy 3. India 4. Elizabeth Fry 5. Gladys Knight
6. Salome 7. Belgium 8. Little Richard 9. Nick Faldo 10. Betty Ford

QUIZ 133

1. What is the first name of the character played by Joanna Lumley in *Absolutely Fabulous*?

2. Which British sitcom ended with Richard marrying Audrey?

3. Which US sitcom saw Alex. Louis, Tony and Latka working for Sunshine Cabs?

4. What is the name of Rodney Trotter's wife in *Only Fools And Horses*?

5. At which holiday camp are Ted Bovis and Gladys Pugh employees?

6. How are Dorothy, Rose, Sophia and Blanche collectively known?

7. Who played the role of Diane Chambers in *Cheers*?

8. Which sitcom featured a married couple called Tom and Barbara who owned a pet goat called Geraldine?

9. What kind of shop did Desmond Ambrose run?

10. What is the name of Martin Crane's pet dog in *Frasier*?

ANSWERS

1. Patsy 2. *To The Manor Born* 3. *Taxi* 4. Cassandra 5. Maplins 6. *The Golden Girls* 7. Shelley Long 8. *The Good Life* 9. Barber shop or hairdressers 10. Eddie

QUIZ 134

. . . .

1 Who was murdered by Baron Fitzurse, Baron Le Breton, Baron De Morville and Baron De Tracy?

2 What is the home state of the Connor family in Roseanne?

3 What is the first name of Miss Jones in *Rising Damp*?

4 Which award-winning series features work colleagues called Dawn Tyndsley and Gareth Keenan?

5 Which US sitcom featured a married couple called Darren and Samantha Stephens?

6 Which comedy couple lived next door to Mr Bickley?

7 Which sitcom featured school pupils called Eric Duffy and Frankie Abbott?

8 In which series did Nigel Hawthorne play Sir Humphrey Appleby?

9 Who played the comic anti-hero Rab C Nesbit?

10 In which comedy series did Craig Charles play Dave Lister?

ANSWERS

1. Thomas Beckett 2. Illinois 3. Ruth 4. *The Office* 5. *Bewitched* 6. Mork and Mindy 7. *Please Sir* 8. *Yes Minister* and *Yes Prime Minister* 9. Gregor Fisher 10. *Red Dwarf*

QUIZ 135

- -

Unravel the anagrams to give the names of ten
    famous singers.

1. MOD NANA
2. ADORN A SIS
3. KORNY GREENS
4. INKY CART RIM
5. CHIC LARD RIFF
6. DULY HOLD BY
7. DATA MAN
8. MOON JETS
9. A ARCHERY AIM
10. SHATTER A EGG

ANSWERS

1. Madonna 2. Diana Ross 3. Kenny Rogers 4. Ricky Martin 5. Cliff Richard
6. Buddy Holly 7. Adam Ant 8. Tom Jones 9. Mariah Carey 10. Gareth Gates

QUIZ 136

. . . .

1   What is the middle name of Elvis Presley?

2   In which year did Mother Teresa die?

3   Which British winter sports hero acquired the nickname of The Eagle?

4   Which group topped the UK charts in 1974 with the song 'Billy Don't Be A Hero'?

5   Who won his 5th consecutive Tour de France in 2003?

6   What connects a hit record for Gerry Rafferty and a thoroughfare for Sherlock Holmes?

7   Who won his 5th consecutive Olympic gold medal at the 2000 Sydney games?

8   Who provided an unlikely duet partner with David Bowie on the 1982 hit 'Little Drummer Boy'?

9   Which evangelist hosted his own radio show entitled *The Hour Of Decision*?

10 Who married Linda Eastman in 1969?

ANSWERS

1. Aaron 2. 1997 3. Eddie Edwards 4. Paper Lace 5. Lance Armstrong
6. Baker Street 7. Steve Redgrave 8. Bing Crosby 9. Billy Graham 10. Paul
McCartney

QUIZ 137

• •

1 Which member of the British royal family penned the children's novel *The Old Man Of Lochnagar*?

2 Who created *Thomas The Tank Engine*?

3 Which grinning feline is a resident of Wonderland?

4 Which diarist returned to the best sellers lists in his cappuccino years?

5 What impractical sailing vessel did Edward Lear's Jumblies use?

6 What is the first name of Lady Chatterley in *Lady Chatterley's Lover*?

7 What is the first name of Lady Chatterley's lover?

8 In which country did Mary Shelley set her novel *Frankenstein*?

9 What kind of animal is Mr Pricklepin in the Beatrix Potter tales?

10 What does the S stand for in the name of the author CS Lewis?

ANSWERS

1. Prince Charles 2. Reverend Awdry 3. The Cheshire Cat 4. Adrian Mole
5. A sieve 6. Constance 7. Oliver 8. Switzerland 9. Porcupine 10. Staples

QUIZ 138

1 Who was the first person to be depicted on a British postage stamp?

2 In the Gulf War of 1991, which general led the US troops in Operation Desert Storm?

3 In which year did Edward VIII abdicate?

4 In which European capital city was the composer Franz Schubert born?

5 Which church was founded by John Wesley?

6 Which monarch was declared insane in 1811?

7 In Roman mythology, who is the king of the gods?

8 In which decade was Sir Walter Raleigh born?

9 What was the name of the plane in which Charles Lindbergh made his first solo flight across the Atlantic?

10 Which US president was nicknamed Old Hickory?

ANSWERS

1. Queen Victoria 2. Norman Schwarzkopf 3. 1936 4. Vienna 5. Methodist
6. George III 7. Jupiter 8. 1550s (1552) 9. The *Spirit of St Louis* 10. Andrew Jackson

QUIZ 139

1 In which Hitchcock thriller did Cary Grant play the role of Roger Thornhill?

2 Who played the title role in the 2002 film *Spiderman*?

3 In which film did Tom Hanks play an insomniac called Sam Baldwin?

4 In which film did John Cleese play a time-obsessed headmaster called John Stimpson?

5 Who carried Fay Wray to the top of the Empire State Building in a 1933 film?

6 Which 1986 film saw Kathleen Turner transported back in time to 1960?

7 What was the title of the second film in which Arnold Schwarzenegger played Conan The Barbarian?

8 In which film did David Niven play 007?

9 Who plays the title role in the 2003 film *The Last Samurai*?

10 In which 1997 film did a giant snake swallow Jon Voight?

ANSWERS

1. *North By Northwest* 2. Toby Maguire 3. *Sleepless In Seattle* 4. *Clockwise*
5. *King Kong* 6. *Peggy Sue Got Married* 7. *Conan The Destroyer* 8. *Casino Royale* 9. Tom Cruise 10. *Anaconda*

QUIZ 140

. . . .

1 Which actor played the father of Harrison Ford in *Indiana Jones And The Last Crusade*?

2 In which film did Geena Davis play the role of Mrs Eleanor Little?

3 Which actor shot dead Robert De Niro in the 1995 film *Heat*?

4 Who played the title role in the comedy drama *My Cousin Vinny*?

5 Which actor played the bad in *The Good, The Bad And The Ugly*?

6 Who did Burt Lancaster portray in *The Gunfight At The OK Corral*?

7 Which 2002 Disney sequel is subtitled Scamps Adventure?

8 Which actor played the role of Marcus Aurelius in *Gladiator*?

9 When Sylvester Stallone played Tango, who played Cash?

10 Who portrayed the first lady of the USA in the sci-fi comedy *Mars Attacks*?

ANSWERS

1. Sean Connery 2. *Stuart Little* 3. Al Pacino 4. Joe Pesci 5. Lee Van Cleef
6. Wyatt Earp 7. *Lady And The Tramp* 2 8. Richard Harris 9. Kurt Russell
10. Glenn Close

QUIZ 141

1 Which century witnessed the first executions of criminals by the electric chair?

2 Which murder suspect in the game of Cluedo shares her name with a bird?

3 Which actor played the title role in the 1976 film *The Outlaw Josey Wales*?

4 Which Olympic skater was found guilty of assaulting her rival Nancy Kerrigan?

5 In 1998 the son of which Cabinet Minister was arrested on suspicion of selling cannabis?

6 Who stole the Queen of Hearts' tarts?

7 Who betrayed Jesus for 30 pieces of silver?

8 In which city did John Christie carry out his murders at 10 Rillington Place?

9 Who was the intended target of The Jackal in the film *The Day Of The Jackal*?

10 In which 1999 film did Tom Hanks portray a death row prison guard called Paul Edgecomb?

ANSWERS

1. 19th century 2. Mrs Peacock 3. Clint Eastwood 4. Tonya Harding
5. Jack Straw 6. The Knave of Hearts 7. Judas 8. London 9. Charles De Gaulle 10. *The Green Mile*

QUIZ 142

1 Who won his seventh Wimbledon title in 2000?

2 Which song has been a hit record for the Righteous Brothers, Robson and Jerome and Gareth Gates?

3 In which park is Princess Diana buried?

4 Which Formula One legend was knighted in the Millennium Honours list?

5 Barbara Gordon is the secret identity of which masked crime fighter?

6 Who was Britain's longest serving prime minister in the 1900s?

7 Which singer is backed by The Commotions?

8 Walter Mondale was the vice president of which US president?

9 Which British footballer was voted European Footballer Of The Year in 2001?

10 In which wing of the White House is the Oval Office of the US President?

ANSWERS

1. Pete Sampras 2. 'Unchained Melody' 3. Althorp Park 4. Stirling Moss
5. Batgirl 6. Margaret Thatcher 7. Lloyd Cole 8. Jimmy Carter 9. Michael
Owen 10. West Wing

QUIZ 143

. . . .

1   What was the title of the US equivalent to *Steptoe And Son*?

2   Who played the title role in the 1990s TV drama Monsignor Renard?

3   Did Columbo, played by Peter Falk, have the first name of Paul, Philip or Patrick?

4   Who played the role of Norm Peterson in *Cheers*?

5   Who played the chalet maid Peggy in *Hi-De-Hi*?

6   Who connects the TV shows *The Bounder*, *Minder* and *Blott On The Landscape*?

7   What is the last name of Phoebe in *Friends*?

8   In which series did Nina Myers kill Teri Bauer?

9   Which popular US comedy series featured the characters of Ralph, Potsie, Joanie and Jenny?

10 Which actor plays the hero in the TV show *Third Rock From The Sun* and the villain in the film *Cliffhanger*?

ANSWERS

1. *Sandford And Son* 2. John Thaw 3. Philip 4. George Wendt 5. Su Pollard
6. George Cole 7. Buffay 8. *24* 9. *Happy Days* 10. John Lithgow

QUIZ 144

• •

In which towns or cities do the following TV characters live?

1 The Boswells in *Bread*

2 Steve McGarrett in *Hawaii 5-0*

3 Inspector Morse

4 Cagney and Lacey

5 The Trotters in *Only Fools And Horses*

6 Tracy and Sharon in *Birds Of A Feather*

7 Van Der Valk

8 McMillan And Wife

9 The Cunninghams in *Happy Days*

10 The Royle family

ANSWERS

1. Liverpool 2. Honolulu 3. Oxford 4. New York 5. Peckham or London
6. Chigwell 7. Amsterdam 8. San Francisco 9. Milwaukee 10. Manchester

QUIZ 145

• •

1 Who was the equine companion of Ricky North?

2 Which marsupial is the best friend of Sonny Hammond?

3 The statue of which horse overlooks the winner's enclosure at Cheltenham racecourse?

4 What is the name of Ron Weasley's pet rat in the *Harry Potter* stories?

5 What is the home town of Rupert The Bear?

6 What kind of animals are the literary characters of Dandelion, Buckthorn and Speedwell?

7 Which dog became a national hero in 1966 after finding the World Cup?

8 Which 1943 film was the first to feature the canine hero Lassie?

9 Who created *Paddington Bear*?

10 Which canary is forever trying to escape the clutches of a cat called Sylvester ?

ANSWERS

1. Champion the Wonder Horse 2. Skippy the Bush Kangaroo 3. Arkle
4. Scabbers 5. Nutwood 6. Rabbits in *Watership Down* 7. Pickles 8. *Lassie Come Home* 9. Michael Bond 10. Tweetie Pie

QUIZ 146

1 What was the nationality of the explorer Mungo Park?

2 In which 1997 film did Nicholas Cage play a prisoner aboard a hijacked plane?

3 What was the first name of King George VI?

4 Which composer acquired the nickname of The Waltz King?

5 Who invented the Spitfire fighter plane?

6 In which decade was Andy Warhol born?

7 Who was the first divorcee to be elected US president?

8 Billy Batson is the secret identity of which superhero?

9 Which Stanley Kubrick film features the outbreak of World War III?

10 Who did Michael Crawford portray on stage when he sang 'Music Of The Night'?

ANSWERS

1. Scottish 2. *Con Air* 3. Albert 4. Johann Strauss 5. Reginald Mitchell
6. 1920s 7. Ronald Reagan 8. Captain Marvel 9. *Dr Strangelove*
10. The Phantom Of The Opera

QUIZ 147

• •

1 Who did the hunchback of Notre Dame fall in love with?

2 Which trio were not afraid of the big bad wolf, despite all his huffing and puffing?

3 What kind of animal is the Beatrix Potter creation Jeremy Fisher?

4 What is the name of the parrot that taught Dr Doolittle to talk to the animals?

5 Which oriental detective hero was created by Earl Biggers?

6 Which former member of the Spice Girls penned an autobiography entitled *Learning To Fly*?

7 Who created the literary detective Nero Wolfe?

8 What is Cathy's surname in *Wuthering Heights*?

9 Which genial uncle narrates the *Brer Rabbit* stories?

10 Shakespeare's Hamlet is the prince of which country?

ANSWERS

1. Esmerelda 2. The three little pigs 3. Frog 4. Polynesia 5. Charlie Chan
6. Posh Spice or Victoria Beckham 7. Rex Stout 8. Earnshaw 9. Uncle Remus
10. Denmark

QUIZ 148

. . . .

1 In which port did Francis Drake "singe the King of Spain's beard"?

2 In 1799, with whom did Horatio Nelson begin a notorious affair?

3 After whom is the Australian state of Tasmania named?

4 Who founded the Raffles hotel in Singapore?

5 Was Alfred the Great's wife called Roseanna, Roxanna or Roberta?

6 Who founded a Communist state in Cuba in 1959?

7 Which king of England died of dysentry in 1422?

8 Who served as president of the USA from 1974 to 1977?

9 Which forest housed the secret hideout of Robin Hood?

10 In which decade did Samuel Pepys begin writing his famed diary?

ANSWERS

1. Cadiz 2. Emma Hamilton 3. Abel Tasman 4. Sir Stamford Raffles
5. Roxanna 6. Fidel Castro 7. Henry V 8. Gerald Ford 9. Sherwood Forest
10. 1660s

QUIZ 149

• •

1 In the 1984 film *The Bounty*, who played Fletcher Christian?

2 Which animated hero married Princess Fiona?

3 In which 2002 film did Tom Hanks play an FBI agent called Carl Hanratty?

4 In which 1998 movie flop did Sean Connery play a villain called Sir August de Winter?

5 Who plays Nearly Headless Nick in the *Harry Potter* movies?

6 Which character created by Chester Gould was played on film by Warren Beatty?

7 In which 1992 film did Deloris Van Cartier become Sister Mary Clarence?

8 When Al Pacino played Johnny, who played Frankie?

9 Which 1990 film co-starred Kiefer Sutherland, Julia Roberts and Kevin Bacon as medical students?

10 In which series of films does Sigourney Weaver play the lead character of Ripley?

ANSWERS

1. Mel Gibson 2. *Shrek* 3. *Catch Me If You Can* 4. *The Avengers* 5. John Cleese
6. Dick Tracy 7. *Sister Act* 8. Michelle Pffeifer 9. *Flatliners* 10. *Alien*

QUIZ 150

. . . .

1   In which 2002 film did Paul Newman play mob boss John Rooney?

2   Which co-creator of *The Muppets* voices the character of Yoda in the *Star Wars* movies?

3   In which film did Jack Lemmon play the roles of Jerry and Daphne?

4   In the second *Die Hard* movie, in which city did John McClane foil a gang of terrorists at an airport?

5   In which Martin Scorsese film did Leonardo Di Caprio play the role of Amsterdam Vallon?

6   In which film did Gary Kemp play the manager of Whitney Houston?

7   Who played the title role in *Dr Zhivago*?

8   Which knighted actor links the films *Ryan's Daughter* and *Scott Of The Antarctic*?

9   Who directed the movie epic *Lawrence Of Arabia*?

10 Which war hero's life story was chronicled in the film *Reach For The Sky*?

ANSWERS

1. *The Road To Perdition* 2. Frank Oz 3. *Some Like It Hot* 4. Washington DC
5. *Gangs Of New York* 6. *The Bodyguard* 7. Omar Sharif 8. Sir John Mills
9. David Lean 10. Douglas Bader

QUIZ 151

1. Which monarch was the intended target of the conspirators of the Gunpowder Plot?

2. Was the rival gang of the Kray twins called the Robertsons, the Redmonds or the Richardsons?

3. Who was executed for treason in 1535, despite holding a knighthood?

4. From which country was Nick Leeson released from prison in 1999?

5. In which sport was Hanse Cronje found guilty of taking bribes?

6. Which Brighton bomber was released from prison in June 1999?

7. In which decade was Mahatma Gandhi assassinated?

8. What was the first name of Rasputin?

9. Which US city was the scene of the Rodney King riots?

10. Who was killed in mysterious circumstances in 1973 and played on film by Meryl Streep ten years later?

ANSWERS

1. James I 2. The Richardsons 3. Sir Thomas More 4. Singapore 5. Cricket
6. Patrick Magee 7. 1940s 8. Grigori 9. Los Angeles 10. Karen Silkwood

QUIZ 152

1 What nationality was Salvador Dali?

2 Who did Ringo Starr replace in The Beatles?

3 Which film directed by Alan Parker tells the story of Eva Peron?

4 From which historical figure did the title of *Kaiser* derive?

5 Which soul legend collaborated with George Michael on the hit record 'I Knew You Were Waiting'?

6 Which school did Tom Brown attend in the novel *Tom Brown's Schooldays*?

7 Which pop trio comprised Morten, Pal and Magna?

8 Which comic strip hero owns a pet dog called Gnasher?

9 What is the secret identity of Batman's sidekick Robin?

10 In Greek mythology, who is the twin sister of Apollo?

ANSWERS

1. Spanish 2. Pete Best 3. *Evita* 4. Julius Caesar 5. Aretha Franklin 6. Rugby
7. A-ha 8. Dennis the Menace 9. Dick Grayson 10. Artemis

QUIZ 153

• •

Identify the TV shows from three of their characters.

1 Joy Merryweather, Henry Davenport, Damien Day

2 Norman Clegg, Foggy Dewhurst, Wally Batty

3 Detective Crocker, Captain McNeil, Detective Stavros

4 Owen the Signal, Idris the Dragon, Evans the Song

5 Jackie Harris, Bucker Brooks, DJ

6 Paulie Gualtieri, Dr Melfi, Uncle Junior

7 Tony Almeida, Kate Warner, David Palmer

8 Lydia Grant, Bruno Martelli, Leroy Johnson

9 Mr Lucas, Mr Rumbold, Captain Peacock

10 Roz Doyle, Bulldog Briscoe, Niles Crane

ANSWERS

1. *Drop The Dead Donkey* 2. *Last Of The Summer Wine* 3. *Kojak* 4. *Ivor the Engine* 5. *Roseanne* 6. *The Sopranos* 7. *24* 8. *Fame* 9. *Are You Being Served?* 10. *Frasier*

QUIZ 154

1 Which former vocalist for Black Sabbath became the star of his own TV reality show?

2 Which writer created the TV hero of DCI Jane Tennison?

3 Who plays the housekeeper Mrs Doyle in *Father Ted*?

4 Which problem solver answers the phone when the number 212 555 4200 is rung?

5 Who plays the role of Petula in the comedy series *Dinnerladies*?

6 In which city is *The Cosby Show* set?

7 Which TV hero is the leader of the Tooting Popular Front?

8 Who played the slow-witted character of the Prince Of Wales in *Blackadder The Third*?

9 Which capital city's name is written on the side of the Trotters' three-wheeler van in *Only Fools And Horses*?

10 What is the name of Mork and Mindy's son?

ANSWERS

1. Ozzy Osbourne 2. Lynda La Plante 3. Pauline McLynn 4. The Equaliser or Robert McCall 5. Julie Walters 6. New York 7. Citizen "Wolfie" Smith
8. Hugh Laurie 9. Paris 10. Mearth

QUIZ 155

1 What is the real first name of Jesse Owens?

2 In which sport did Errol Flynn compete in the Olympics?

3 Which Irish swimmer won three gold medals at the 1996 Olympics?

4 In 1964, which Ethiopian runner became the first person to win the Olympic marathon on two occasions?

5 Which Olympic hero was portrayed by Ben Cross in the film *Chariots Of Fire*?

6 Which year saw the athletes Ben Johnson stripped of his Olympic title?

7 Which US athlete collected a total of four gold medals at the 1984 Summer Olympics?

8 Which female athlete lit the Olympic flame at the 2000 Sydney Games?

9 Who accidentally tripped Mary Decker in a 1984 Olympic final?

10 In which sport was Dawn Fraser crowned champion in three successive Olympics?

ANSWERS

1. James 2. Boxing 3. Michelle Smith 4. Abebe Bikila 5. Harold Abrahams
6. 1988 7. Carl Lewis 8. Cathy Freeman 9. Zola Budd 10. Swimming

QUIZ 156

. . . .

1 In the Bible, who is the mother of the Virgin Mary?

2 Which partner of Fred Astaire died in 1995?

3 Who succeeded John F Kennedy as US president?

4 What nationality is the tennis star Ilie Nastase?

5 Which duo composed The Savoy Operas?

6 Who is the daughter of Hippolyte, Queen of the Amazons?

7 Which former England cricket captain is nicknamed Beefy?

8 Which awards were named after Antoinette Perry?

9 Which fictional character drove a Rolls Royce called The Grey Panther?

10 Which football manager's 1999 autobiography is entitled *Managing My Life*?

ANSWERS

1. Anne 2. Ginger Rogers 3. Lyndon B Johnson 4. Romanian 5. Gilbert and Sullivan 6. Wonder Woman 7. Ian Botham 8. The Tonys 9. Sexton Blake 10. Alex Ferguson

QUIZ 157

• •

1   Who was the first stepmother of Elizabeth I?

2   How many times did Peter deny Jesus Christ?

3   Which monarch died at the Battle of Bosworth Field?

4   In what year did Nadia Comaneci become the first gymnast to score a perfect 10?

5   In which country was Marie Antoinette born?

6   Who was the father of the legendary King Arthur?

7   In the Bible, whose wife was turned into a pillar of salt?

8   In the 1860s, Captain Briggs skippered which sailing vessel?

9   Who was the first US president to win the Nobel Peace Prize?

10 Of which native American tribe was Geronimo the chief?

ANSWERS

1. Jane Seymour 2. Three times 3. Richard III 4. 1976 5. Austria 6. Uther Pendragon 7. Lot's wife 8. *Marie Celeste* 9. Theodore Roosevelt 10. Apache

QUIZ 158

. . . .

1   Which film saw the young hero Kevin McAllister battling against a pair of hapless housebreakers?

2   Which stetson-wearing screen hero was born Leonard Franklin Slye?

3   Who was the first actor to play Hannibal Lecter on film?

4   Who played the role of Jinx in the Bond movie *Die Another Day*?

5   Which Hollywood superstar voiced the character of John Smith in the animated movie *Pocahontas*?

6   Which film marked the screen farewells of Clark Gable and Marilyn Monroe?

7   Which American hero was portrayed by Ronald Reagan in the film *Santa Fe Trail*?

8   What type of weather is associated with the film character of Don Lockwood?

9   Sally Bowles is the lead character in which award-winning musical?

10 In the 1994 film *The Flintstones*, which Bedrock resident was played by Rosie O'Donnell?

ANSWERS

1. *Home Alone* 2. Roy Rogers 3. Brian Cox 4. Halle Berry 5. Mel Gibson
6. *The Misfits* 7. General George Custer 8. Rain (lead character in *Singing In The Rain*) 9. *Cabaret* 10. Betty Rubble

QUIZ 159

• •

1 In which 1996 film did Jack Nicholson play the president of the USA?

2 Which evil lord is voiced by John Lithgow in the film *Shrek*?

3 Who replaced Jodie Foster in the film role of Clarice Starling?

4 In which animated film did John Goodman voice the character of Sulley?

5 In which Oscar-winning film did Colin Firth play Lord Wessex and Judi Dench play Queen Elizabeth I?

6 Which director links the films *Mississippi Burning*, *Fame* and *The Commitments*?

7 Who plays the wife of Jim Carrey in the film *Bruce Almighty*?

8 Who plays the role of God in the film *Bruce Almighty*?

9 In which 1999 film did Denzel Washington play a boxer called Reubin Carter?

10 In which film did Whoopi Goldberg play a medium called Oda Mae Brown?

ANSWERS

1. *Mars Attacks* 2. Lord Farquaad 3. Julianne Moore 4., *Monsters Inc*
5. *Shakespeare In Love* 6. Alan Parker 7. Jennifer Aniston 8. Morgan Freeman
9. *The Hurricane* 10. *Ghost*

QUIZ 160

1 Which city witnessed the St Valentine's Day Massacre?

2 In which novel and film did James Bond foil a plot to rob Fort Knox?

3 Who, nicknamed The Godfather of Soul, received a jail sentence in 1988 for firearms offences?

4 Which horse won the Derby in 1981 and was kidnapped two years later?

5 Which Italian prime minister was assassinated by the Red Brigades in 1978?

6 In which year was Lord Mountbatten assassinated?

7 Which gangster was portrayed by Christian Slater in the 1991 film *Mobsters*?

8 In which bay were the first convict settlements in Australia established?

9 In 1977, which group was arrested on a boat on the river Thames while performing 'God Save The Queen'?

10 Uxoricide is the crime of killing one's what?

ANSWERS

1. Chicago 2. *Goldfinger* 3. James Brown 4. Shergar 5. Aldo Moro 6. 1979
7. Lucky Luciano 8. Botany Bay 9. The Sex Pistols 10. Wife

QUIZ 161

1 Who narrates the *Sherlock Holmes* tales?

2 What is the name of Billy Bunter's sister?

3 Who died while writing *The Mystery Of Edwin Drood*?

4 Who created the storybook character of Willy Wonka?

5 In which city was the author Sir Walter Scott born?

6 What day of the week did Robinson Crusoe name his desert island companion after?

7 *Jude The Obscure* was the last novel of which author?

8 Who penned the novel *Catch 22*?

9 On which island was Ben Gunn marooned?

10 Which author links the novels *Fever Pitch* and *About A Boy*?

ANSWERS

1. Dr Watson 2. Bessie 3. Charles Dickens 4. Roald Dahl 5. Edinburgh
6. Friday 7. Thomas Hardy 8. Joseph Heller 9. Treasure Island 10. Nick
Hornby

QUIZ 162

1 What was the original surname of civil rights leader Malcolm X?

2 Who relieved Muhammed Ali of his world title in 1978?

3 Which manager of The Beatles died in 1967?

4 In which month is St Patrick's Day celebrated?

5 Who was sacked as England's soccer manager in 1974?

6 In which country was the singer/songwriter Paul Anka born?

7 Which member of the Rat Pack died on Christmas Day 1995?

8 In 2002 who recorded the best-selling album *Escapology*?

9 Which island is home to Zorba the Greek?

10 Under what name did Harry Webb record several chart-topping singles?

ANSWERS

1. Little 2. Leon Spinx 3. Brian Epstein 4. March 5. Alf Ramsey 6. Canada
7. Dean Martin 8. Robbie Williams 9. Crete 10. Cliff Richard

QUIZ 163

1 Who has dated Aunt Sally, Saucy Nancy and Dolly Clothespeg?

2 What is the first name of Captain Mainwaring in *Dad's Army*?

3 Texas Pete is the archenemy of which ursine hero on children's TV?

4 Which duo present the TV shows *Pop Idol* and *I'm A Celebrity, Get Me Out Of Here*?

5 In which city does the TV hero Fitz work in the drama series *Cracker*?

6 Which 1960s series saw the heroic David Vincent battling against aliens?

7 Which member of *The Goodies* wore a Union Jack waistcoat?

8 Which US series featured a pair of doberman guard dogs called Zeus and Apollo?

9 Which animated skunk first appeared in a cartoon entitled *Odor-able Kitty*?

10 Which role did Andrew Sachs play in *Fawlty Towers*?

ANSWERS

1. Worzel Gummidge 2. George 3. Superted 4. Ant and Dec 5. Manchester
6. *The Invaders* 7. Tim Brooke-Taylor 8. *Magnum PI* 9. Pepe Le Pew
10. Manuel

QUIZ 164

. . . .

1 What type of building did Jonathan Creek make his home?

2 Who is the alter ego of the spoof chat-show hostess Mrs Merton?

3 Who plays the role of June Monsoon in *Absolutely Fabulous*?

4 What car does Mr Bean drive?

5 What colour is the beard of the cartoon character Yosemite Sam?

6 Who plays the male half of Terry and June?

7 What model of Ford car did Starsky and Hutch drive?

8 In which comedy series did Judi Dench co-star with her husband Michael Williams?

9 Who plays the role of Malcolm in *Malcolm In The Middle*?

10 Who plays the role of Wiliam T Ryker in *Star Trek:The Next Generation*?

ANSWERS

1. A windmill 2. Caroline Aherne 3. June Whitfield 4. Mini 5. Red 6. Terry Scott 7. Torino 8. *A Fine Romance* 9. Frankie Muniz 10. Jonathan Frakes

QUIZ 165

. . . .

1 Who created *The Grinch*?

2 Which Ancient Greek physician is known as the Father of Medicine?

3 Which Irishman founded his first home for homeless boys in 1870?

4 Which film role links Rex Harrison and Eddie Murphy?

5 Which 1993 film saw Dr Alan Grant battling against dinosaurs?

6 Who performed the first successful heart transplant operation in 1967?

7 Which actor plays the role of Dr McCoy in *Star Trek*?

8 Who is the archenemy of Austin Powers?

9 Who was executed in 1910 for the murder of his wife Cora?

10 Which film villain was played in 1962 by Joseph Wiseman?

ANSWERS

1. Dr Seuss 2. Hippocrates 3. Dr Barnardo 4. Dr Doolittle 5. Jurassic Park
6. Dr Christiaan Barnard 7. DeForest Kelley 8. Dr Evil 9. Dr Crippen
10. Dr No

QUIZ 166

1 Who, born Virginia Pugh, became a leading light in country and western music?

2 What is the middle name of Ronald Reagan?

3 Which singer had 1990s hits with the songs 'She Bangs' and 'Private Emotion'?

4 Which artist had the surname of Buonarotti?

5 Which former world snooker champion acquired the nickname of Dracula?

6 Which Irish rock star was born George Ivan?

7 Which song did Cliff Richard sing when he first represented the UK in the Eurovision Song Contest?

8 Who topped the charts as a 52 year old with the song 'Believe'?

9 Who is Shakespeare's King of the Fairies?

10 Who is Shakespeare's Queen of the Fairies?

ANSWERS

1. Tammy Wynette 2. Wilson 3. Ricky Martin 4. Michelangelo 5. Ray Reardon 6. Van Morrison 7. 'Congratulations' 8. Cher 9. Oberon 10. Titania

QUIZ 167

. . . .

1 The book *The Voyage Of The Beagle* chronicled the discoveries of which scientist?

2 Which septet is accompanied by a dog called Scamper?

3 The hero Tom Canty features in which adventure novel?

4 What does Dr Griffin discover the secret of in a story by HG Wells?

5 Who penned the Pulitzer Prize-winning novel *The Color Purple*?

6 Which male first name is included in the title of seven Shakespeare plays?

7 What is the name of AA Milne's son?

8 Becky Sharpe is the heroine of which novel?

9 What type of animals are the storybook characters Babar and Celeste?

10 John Harmon is the character referred to in the title of which Dickens novel?

ANSWERS

1. Charles Darwin 2. The Secret Seven 3. *The Prince And The Pauper*
4. Invisibility 5. Alice Walker 6. Henry 7. Christopher Robin 8. *Vanity Fair*
9. Elephants 10. *Our Mutual Friend*

QUIZ 168

. . . .

1 In which century was the composer Franz Schubert born?

2 Which nation has provided the greatest number of popes?

3 What was the name of George Bush Senior's wife and first lady?

4 From 51BC to 30BC who was known as The Queen of the Nile?

5 Which US president did Winston Churchill meet at the Casablanca Conference in 1943?

6 Who was the first British monarch to live at Buckingham Palace?

7 Who did Henry Morton Stanley travel to Africa in search of?

8 Which US president officially opened the Panama Canal?

9 At which battle was Horatio Nelson fatally wounded?

10 Which bloodthirsty leader of the Mongol empire died in 1227?

ANSWERS

1. 18th 2. Italy 3. Barbara 4. Cleopatra 5. Franklin D Roosevelt 6. Queen Victoria 7. Dr Livingstone 8. Woodrow Wilson 9. The Battle of Trafalgar 10. Genghis Khan

QUIZ 169

1. Who played the role of Breathless Mahoney in *Dick Tracy*?

2. In which 1994 film did Bruce Willis play a boxer called Butch Coolidge?

3. In which 1988 film did Arnold Schwarzenegger and Danny DeVito play a pair of unlikely brothers?

4. Which sport features in the film *The Legend Of Bagger Vance*?

5. Who played the title role in the 1953 film *Shane*?

6. From which country does the Disney folk-hero Mulan hail?

7. Which role is played by Michelle Pfeifer in *Batman Returns*?

8. Who overcame her deafness to win an Oscar for her role in the film *Children Of A Lesser God*?

9. Which character spoke the last line of the film *Gone With The Wind*?

10. Which 1994 film co-starred Mel Gibson and Jodie Foster as Bret and Annabelle?

ANSWERS

1. Madonna 2. *Pulp Fiction* 3. *Twins* 4. Golf 5. Alan Ladd 6. China
7. Catwoman 8. Marlee Matlin 9. Scarlet O'Hara 10. *Maverick*

QUIZ 170

. . . .

Who plays the following roles in the *Star Wars* movies?

1 Count Dooku

2 Qui-Gonn Jinn

3 Chancellor Valorum

4 Luke Skywalker

5 Padme Amidala

6 Boss Nass

7 Mace Windu

8 Princess Leia

9 Obi-Wan Kenobi as an old man

10 Obi-Wan Kenobi as a young man

ANSWERS

1. Christopher Lee 2. Liam Neeson 3. Terence Stamp 4. Mark Hamill
5. Natalie Portman 6. Brian Blessed 7. Samuel L Jackson 8. Carrie Fisher
9. Alec Guinness 10. Ewan McGregor

QUIZ 171

1 Which British monarch was excommunicated by Pope Paul III?

2 Hanged in 1949, what nickname was given to the killer John George Haigh?

3 In 1969 the country and western star Johnny Cash recorded a famous album in which prison?

4 Which *Carry On* film saw Sid James playing a highwayman?

5 From which London embassy were 26 hostages rescued by the SAS in 1980?

6 In the 1970s which MP for Walsall was jailed after faking his own death?

7 In which city was Gianni Versace murdered?

8 Which Scandinavian prime minister was assassinated in February 1986?

9 Which Motown legend was arrested at Heathrow Airport in 1999 after objecting to a body search?

10 Which Beatle was attacked by a knife-wielding intruder in December 1999?

ANSWERS

1. Henry VIII 2. The Acid Bath Murderer 3. San Quentin 4. *Carry On Dick*
5. Iranian Embassy 6. John Stonehouse 7. Miami 8. Olaf Palme 9. Diana
Ross 10. George Harrison

QUIZ 172

. . . .

1 Who was crowned Mr Universe in 1968, before finding fame in the world of film and politics?

2 What is the name of Charlie Brown's pet dog?

3 How were Peter Sellers, Michael Bentine, Spike Milligan and Harry Secombe collectively known?

4 Which mythological hero killed the monster Grendel?

5 What form of cancer was named after the physicist who isolated it in 1832?

6 Who has been played on TV by Hugh O'Brian and on film by Kurt Russell and Kevin Costner?

7 Who found the Holy Grail in Arthurian legend?

8 Who was the first Roman Catholic to be elected president of the USA?

9 Who was the last English monarch to be executed?

10 Which operatic heroine was stabbed to death by Don José?

ANSWERS

1. Arnold Schwarzenegger 2. Snoopy 3. The Goons 4. Beowulf
5. Hodgkin's Disease 6. Wyatt Earp 7. Sir Galahad 8. John F Kennedy
9. Charles I 10. Carmen

QUIZ 173

. . . .

1 Which pop legend was the subject of the TV documentary *Tantrums And Tiaras*?

2 What is the name of the son of Gomez and Morticia Addams?

3 Which superhero worked for the Foundation For Oceanic Research?

4 Which captain was possessed by the Mysterons in *Captain Scarlet*?

5 On whose TV show did The Beatles make their US TV debut?

6 Who played Polly Sherman in *Fawlty Towers* and also co-wrote the series?

7 Which actor played the title role in *Banacek*?

8 What is the name of Jim Royle's local pub in *The Royle Family*?

9 Which series sees Ross sipping coffee at the Central Perk coffee bar?

10 Who played the male half of Dempsey and Makepeace?

ANSWERS

1. Elton John 2. Pugsley 3. Man From Atlantis 4. Captain Black 5. Ed Sullivan 6. Connie Booth 7. George Peppard 8. The Feathers 9. *Friends* 10. Michael Brandon

QUIZ 174

Identify the TV comedy shows from two of their
characters.

1   Bishop Brennan and Jack Hackett

2   Jethro Bodine and Mr Drysdale

3   Spike Dixon and Fred Quilly

4   Private Doberman and Corporal Fender

5   Cosmo Kramer and George Costanza

6   Rupert Rigsby and Philip Smith

7   Captain Darling and Bob

8   Ned Flanders and Barney Gumble

9   Private Walker and Mavis Pike

10 Jerry St Clair and Keith Lard

ANSWERS

1. *Father Ted* 2. *The Beverly Hillbillies* 3. *Hi-De-Hi* 4. *Sergeant Bilko* aka *The Phil
Silvers Show* 5. *Seinfeld* 6. *Rising Damp* 7. *Blackadder Goes Forth*
8. *The Simpsons* 9. *Dad's Army* 10. *Phoenix Nights*

QUIZ 175

. . . .

1 Who piloted *Fireball XL5*?

2 The Draconians are the chief adversaries of which 25th-century hero?

3 Which space-age hero has the catchphrase "To infinity and beyond"?

4 Whose girlfriend is called Dale Arden?

5 Which *Star Wars* character was voiced by James Earl Jones?

6 In which sci-fi series did Lorne Greene play Commander Adama?

7 Who has battled against the Cybermen, the Ice Warriors and the Sea Devils?

8 Which lieutenant on the USS Enterprise is played by Michael Dorn?

9 Whom did Harrison Ford portray in three *Star Wars* movies?

10 Which sci-fi series featured Dr Zachary Smith as the villain and the Robinson family as the heroes?

ANSWERS

1. Steve Zodiac 2. Buck Rogers 3. Buzz Lightyear 4. Flash Gordon 5. Darth Vader 6. *Battlestar Galactica* 7. Dr Who 8. Lieutenant Worf 9. Han Solo 10. *Lost In Space*

QUIZ 176

. . . .

1 What is the name of the wife of the Greek hero Ulysses?

2 Whom did Wisden's Almanac vote as their number-one cricketer of the 20th century?

3 Which soul legend was backed by The Miracles?

4 What is the nationality of the tennis star Kim Clijsters?

5 Who was elected Chancellor of Germany in 1982?

6 Who did Paul McCartney marry at Castle Leslie?

7 After which goddess is the capital of Greece named?

8 Baden-Powell House is the headquarters of which organisation?

9 Which cocktail was named after a US surfer called Tom Harvey?

10 What was the real first name of Bob Hope?

ANSWERS

1. Penelope 2. Donald Bradman 3. Smokey Robinson 4. Belgian 5. Helmut Kohl 6. Heather Mills 7. Athene 8. Boy Scouts 9. Harvey Wallbanger 10. Leslie

QUIZ 177

• •

1 Who created the Napoleonic War hero *Sharpe*?

2 Who wrote the book *Diana: Her True Story*?

3 What is the name of the policeman in the *Noddy* stories?

4 Who, after being released from captivity, wrote a book entitled *Taken On Trust*?

5 What is the nationality of the author of *Peter Pan*?

6 On whose book did Andrew Lloyd Webber base his stage musical *Cats*?

7 Who penned *The Ballad Of Reading Gaol*?

8 What type of food did Oliver Twist ask for more of?

9 Who created the character of Katy Carr in the *What Katy Did* series of children's novels?

10 Which Belgian novelist created the Parisian detective Maigret?

ANSWERS

QUIZ 178

. . . .

1 The name of which Roman emperor means 'little boots'?

2 Which angel foretold the birth of Jesus Christ?

3 In which English county was Francis Drake born?

4 After whom is the country of Bolivia named?

5 In which country did the Duke of Wellington lead his troops at the Battle of Waterloo?

6 Did Robert the Bruce die of leprosy, the Black Death or tubercolosis?

7 How many US presidents preceded George Bush Jnr: 40, 41 or 42?

8 How old was King Arthur when he pulled the sword Excalibur from the stone: 14, 15 or 16?

9 In which year did Hitler invade Poland?

10 Which French monarch was known as the Sun King?

ANSWERS

1. Caligula 2. Gabriel 3. Devon 4. Simon Bolivar 5. Belgium 6. Leprosy 7. 42
8. 15 9. 1939 10. Louis XIV

QUIZ 179

1 If all the Bond movies are listed alphabetically, which comes last?

2 Which actor who played the evil Dr Phibes on film died in 1993?

3 Who played the Artful Dodger when Ron Moody played Fagin?

4 Who did Gregory Peck portray in the film *Moby Dick*?

5 The 1970 film *Song Of Norway* told the story of which classical composer?

6 Which blues legend was portrayed by Diana Ross in *Lady Sings The Blues*?

7 Which film star is the mother of the film star Kate Hudson?

8 Which campanologist has been portrayed on film by Lon Chaney, Charles Laughton and Anthony Quinn?

9 Who plays the role of Natalie Cook in the 2000 film version of *Charlie's Angels*?

10 Which young man cub is befriended by Baloo the bear in *The Jungle Book*?

ANSWERS

1. *You Only Live Twice* 2. Vincent Price 3. Jack Wild 4. Captain Ahab
5. Edvard Grieg 6. Billie Holliday 7. Goldie Hawn 8. Quasimodo 9. Cameron Diaz 10. Mowgli

QUIZ 180

1 Which superhero is played on film by Hugh Jackman in *X-Men*?

2 Which one-legged villain has been played on film by Orson Welles and Robert Newton?

3 Who played the superhero Daredevil in a 2003 box office flop?

4 In which film did the heroic Volkswagen *Herbie* first appear?

5 What is Al short for in the name of Al Pacino?

6 In which film did George Kennedy win an Oscar for his portrayal of a character called Dragline?

7 In which movie did Sylvester Stallone rescue a group of people trapped inside Manhatten's Holland Tunnel?

8 Who played the role of President Marshall in *Airforce One*?

9 Which movie mogul was portrayed by Dan Aykroyd in the film *Chaplin*?

10 In the film *Thelma And Louise*, did Susan Sarandon play Thelma or Louise?

ANSWERS

1. Wolverine 2. Long John Silver 3. Ben Affleck 4. *The Love Bug* 5. Alfredo 6. *Cool Hand Luke* 7. *Daylight* 8. Harrison Ford 9. Mack Sennett 10. Louise

QUIZ 181

1 In which prison was *The Man In The Iron Mask* incarcerated for five years?

2 What was stolen by Scottish Nationalists from Westminster Abbey in 1950?

3 Which decade witnessed the last execution carried out in Britain?

4 Which basketball superstar's father was murdered in 1993?

5 In which prison was the literary character Moll Flanders born?

6 In which year was WPC Yvonne Fletcher shot dead outside the Libyan Embassy in London?

7 Whose 45-year old-murder conviction was overturned in 1998?

8 In 1877, Frank Cahill became whose first victim?

9 What canine nickname was given to the gangster Vincent Coll?

10 In which country was Bobby Moore arrested following false theft charges prior to the 1970 World Cup?

ANSWERS

1. The Bastille 2. The Stone Of Scone 3. 1960s 4. Michael Jordan
5. Newgate Prison 6. 1984 7. Derek Bentley 8. Billy the Kid 9. Mad Dog
10. Colombia

QUIZ 182

• •

1 Whom did Margaret Thatcher replace as leader of the Conservative Party?

2 Who designed the Eiffel Tower?

3 Which 1960s singing star received backing vocals from the Pacemakers?

4 Which mythological hero had to carry out 12 labours, including capturing the Cretan Bull?

5 Which rock music legend married the supermodel Iman in 1992?

6 In which sport did Alison Fisher become the ladies world champion?

7 Who was the first South African golfer to win the US Open?

8 In which city did the Pope survive an assassination attempt in 1981?

9 Which artist went through a blue period, a pink period and a brown period?

10 Which entertainer penned an autobiography entitled *Can You Tell What It Is Yet*?

ANSWERS

1. Edward Heath 2. Gustav Eiffel 3. Gerry Marsden 4. Hercules 5. David Bowie 6. Snooker 7. Gary Player 8. Rome 9. Pablo Picasso 10. Rolf Harris

QUIZ 183

1. Who played the role of Terry Collier in *The Likely Lads*?

2. Which 1960s comedy featured the characters of Colonel Klink and Colonel Hogan?

3. Under which building is the Batcave located?

4. Which series features the characters of Albert Moxey and Barry Taylor?

5. Which series featured a corrupt politician called Boss Hogg?

6. Which man of the cloth was played on TV by Alexander Guage and on film by Mike McShane?

7. Who composed the theme music for *Miami Vice*?

8. What is the first name of Blake in *Blake's Seven*?

9. For which series did Dennis Waterman perform the theme song 'I Could Be So Good For You'?

10. Thadeus Jones was the alias of which outlaw in *Alias Smith And Jones*?

ANSWERS

1. James Bolam 2. *Hogan's Heroes* 3. Wayne Manor 4. *Auf Wiedersehen Pet*
5. *The Dukes Of Hazzard* 6. Friar Tuck 7. Jan Hammer 8. Roj 9. *Minder*
10. Kid Curry

QUIZ 184

• •

1. In which series does Paul Gross play a Canadian mountie called Benton Fraser?

2. Who links the TV shows *The New Statesman* and *The Young Ones*?

3. What is the name of Del Boy's son in *Only Fools And Horses*?

4. What type of animal is Colonel K, the boss of Dangermouse?

5. What does the BA stand for with regard to the *A Team* character BA Baracus?

6. In which sci-fi series did Jane Badler play an evil alien called Diana?

7. Who played the role of Lennie Godber in *Porridge*?

8. What is the first name of Sergeant Bilko?

9. Who played the title role in *Father Ted*?

10. Who played Josh Randall in *Wanted Dead Or Alive* and went on to become a major Hollywood star?

ANSWERS

1. *Due South* 2. Rik Mayall 3. Damian 4. Walrus 5. Bad Attitude 6. *V*
7. Richard Beckinsale 8. Ernest 9. Dermot Morgan 10. Steve McQueen

QUIZ 185

• •

1 Which Falklands War hero's autobiography is entitled *Walking Tall*?

2 Did Horatio Nelson lose his left or right eye?

3 Which war hero was portrayed by Richard Todd in the film *The Dam Busters*?

4 Who is buried beneath the Arc de Triomphe?

5 The film *To Hell And Back* was based on the autobiography of which highly decorated American war hero?

6 Which poet, killed in World War I, penned the poem 'The Soldier'?

7 In which Oscar-winning film did Alec Guinness play the role of Colonel Nicholson?

8 Which British naval hero was referred to as 'The Dragon' by the Spanish?

9 Which general led the US troops at the 1812 Battle of New Orleans?

10 Who refused an Oscar for his portrayal of General Patton?

ANSWERS

1. Simon Weston 2. Right eye 3. Guy Gibson 4. The Unknown Soldier
5. Audie Murphy 6. Rupert Brooke 7. *Bridge On The River Kwai* 8. Francis
Drake 9. Andrew Jackson 10. George C Scott

QUIZ 186

1 What year marked the deaths of the pop heroes Elvis Presley and Marc Bolan?

2 In 1999 who was voted Sexiest Woman of the Century by *People* magazine?

3 Which pop star's songs feature in the stage musical *Tonight's The Night*?

4 Diane Prince is the secret identity of who?

5 Which group won the Eurovision Song Contest in 1974?

6 In which capital city was Leon Trotsky assassinated?

7 What letter of the alphabet is depicted on the costume of the Boy Wonder, the sidekick of Batman?

8 Who is the Greek counterpart of the Roman goddess Venus?

9 What name connects the horses of Ernie the fastest milkman in the west and Roy Rogers?

10 In which sport were the great rivals Helen Wills Moody and Helen Jacobs known as The Two Helens?

ANSWERS

1. 1977 2. Marilyn Monroe 3. Rod Stewart 4. Wonder Woman 5. Abba
6. Mexico City 7. R for Robin 8. Aphrodite 9. Trigger 10. Tennis

QUIZ 187

• •

Unravel the anagrams to give the names of ten
   famous authors.

1 SWILL OR CLEAR

2 JOLLY COPIER

3 A CLENCHERS SKID

4 HAD DOLLAR

5 CLATTER SWOT

6 FIND SICK CAR

7 DEBIT NYLON

8 INFLAME GIN

9 FLOWING VIA RIO

10 DRAW DEALER

ANSWERS

1. Lewis Carroll 2. Jilly Cooper 3. Charles Dickens 4. Roald Dahl 5. Walter
Scott 6. Dick Francis 7. Enid Blyton 8. Ian Fleming 9. Virginia Woolf
10. Edward Lear

QUIZ 188

1 What was the original name of Francis Drake's flagship the *Golden Hind*?

2 Who went in search of El Dorado after being released from the Tower of London in 1616?

3 How many times had Mrs Wallis Simpson been married before her wedding to Edward VIII?

4 Which Russian statesman won the Nobel Peace Prize in 1990?

5 Who on his arrival in New York said "I have nothing to declare but my genius"?

6 Which Italian city was ruled by the Medici family?

7 Who committed suicide in 399BC with a fatal dose of hemlock?

8 From which English county did the Tolpuddle Martyrs hail?

9 Whom did Winston Churchill describe as "a sheep in sheep's clothing"?

10 Which mad monk was murdered by a group of Russian aristocrats in December 1916?

ANSWERS

1. The *Pelican* 2. Sir Walter Raleigh 3. Twice 4. Mikhail Gorbachev 5. Oscar Wilde 6. Florence 7. Socrates 8. Dorset 9. Clement Atlee 10. Rasputin

QUIZ 189

- -

1   Which rock legend links the films *Dune*, *The Bride* and *Plenty*?

2   In which series of films does Tom Cruise play an all-action hero called Ethan Hunt?

3   How were Chevy Chase, Martin Short and Steve Martin collectively known in the title of a 1986 film?

4   What was invented, driven and flown by Caractacus Potts?

5   Which actor got stung in *The Sting* and eaten alive in *Jaws*?

6   What is the name of Beauty in Disney's animated version of *Beauty And The Beast*?

7   What is the first name of the film hero Rambo?

8   In which film did Robin Williams play an adult Peter Pan?

9   Who played Count Dracula in the comedy film *Dracula: Dead And Loving It*?

10 Which Bond girl was played by Honor Blackman?

ANSWERS

1. Sting 2. *Mission Impossible* 3. *The Three Amigoes* 4. *Chitty Chitty Bang Bang*
5. Robert Shaw 6. Belle 7. John 8. *Hook* 9. Leslie Nielsen 10. *Pussy Galore*

QUIZ 190

1. In which 1999 film did Julia Roberts suffer from an aversion to walking down the aisle?

2. Who won a Best Director Oscar for the Vietnam War movie *Platoon*?

3. Which furry villains do Mogwais turn into if fed after midnight?

4. Which actor partnered Will Smith in the films *Bad Boys* and *Bad Boys II*?

5. Which screen legend links the films *The African Queen*, *On Golden Pond* and *Woman Of The Year*?

6. Which role is played by Snoop Dog in the 2004 big screen version of *Starsky And Hutch*?

7. Which film co-starred Tara Fitzgerald and Ewan McGregor as members of a colliery band?

8. Who played King Arthur in the 1995 film *First Knight*?

9. Which British Prime Minister was portrayed by Anthony Hopkins in the film *Young Winston*?

10. Who played the title role in the first Hollywood production of *Dracula*?

ANSWERS

1. Runaway Bride 2. Oliver Stone 3. Gremlins 4. Martin Lawrence
5. Katharine Hepburn 6. Huggy Bear 7. Brassed Off 8. Sean Connery
9. David Lloyd George 10. Bela Lugosi

QUIZ 191

1. In which year of the 1990s was Monica Seles stabbed on court by a deranged fan of Steffi Graf?

2. In which film did Dustin Hoffman and Robert Redford play the journalists who uncovered the Watergate plot?

3. Who was the driver of the car in which the passenger Mary Jo Kopechne was killed in 1969?

4. Who did Marvin Gaye Snr shoot dead in 1984?

5. The murdered Richard Ramirez, known as the Night Stalker, terrorized which US city in the 1980s?

6. Who acquired the nickname of Suicide Sal from a poem that she wrote?

7. In which film, based on a true story, did Jeremy Irons play the murder suspect Claus Von Bulow?

8. The Duke of Clarence and Prince Albert were both suspected of being which criminal?

9. In which wild west town were the McLowery brothers and Bill Clanton shot dead?

10. What weapon gave the gangster George Kelly his nickname?

ANSWERS

1. 1993 2. *All The President's Men* 3. Edward Kennedy 4. His son Marvin Gaye Jnr 5. Los Angeles 6. Bonnie Parker 7. *Reversal Of Fortune* 8. Jack the Ripper 9. Tombstone 10. Machine gun .

QUIZ 192

. . . .

1   Which part of Peter Pan was kept in a drawer?

2   Who sailed around the world in a yacht called
    Kingfisher?

3   Which college was founded by Henry VI in 1440?

4   Who was elected lord mayor of London in 2000?

5   Which pop group's music features in the West End
    musical *We Will Rock You*?

6   The 1999 TV documentary *Bring Me Sunshine*
    chronicled the work of which comedian?

7   In what year did Yuri Gagarin become the first
    man in space?

8   Who received an honorary knighthood in 1986
    after organizing Live Aid?

9   Which inventor of the mini skirt said " A woman is
    as young as her knee"?

10 Who produced the Michael Jackson album
    Thriller?

ANSWERS

1. His shadow 2. Ellen MacArthur 3. Eton 4. Ken Livingstone 5. Queen
6. Eric Morecambe 7. 1961 8. Bob Geldof 9. Mary Quant 10. Quincy Jones

QUIZ 193

Identify the children's TV show from the characters given.

1 Benny the Ball, Spook and Fancy

2 Chippy Minton, Micky Murphy, Dibble and Grubb

3 Big Bird and Oscar the Grouch

4 Lieutenant Ninety, Commander Zero and Robert the Robot

5 Zsa Zsa and Miss Kiki Frog

6 Dill the Dog, Parsley the Lion, Sage the Owl

7 Mr Rusty, Dougal and Florence

8 Fleegle, Bingo, Drooper and Snorky

9 Tobermory and Orinoco

10 Fred, Daphne and Velma

ANSWERS

1. *Top Cat* 2. *Trumpton* 3. *Sesame Street* 4. *Fireball XL5* 5. *Hector's House*
6. *The Herbs* 7. *The Magic Roundabout* 8. *Banana Splits* 9. *The Wombles*
10. *Scooby Doo*

QUIZ 194

• •

Who performed the theme songs for the following
  shows?

1 *Rawhide*

2 *Whatever Happened To The Likely Lads?*

3 *The Wonder Years*

4 *The Royle Family*

5 *Dad's Army*

6 *Moonlighting*

7 *Frasier*

8 *Friends*

9 *One Foot In The Grave*

10 *Ally McBeal*

ANSWERS

1. Frankie Laine 2. Manfred Mann 3. Joe Cocker 4. Oasis 5. Bud Flanagan
6. Al Jarreau 7. Kelsey Grammar 8. The Rembrandts 9. Eric Idle 10. Vonda
Shepard

QUIZ 195

1 Thetis is the mother of which mythological hero?

2 Which month of the year is named after a two-faced god?

3 Who killed the gorgon Medusa?

4 Name the father of Icarus, who built the labyrinth on the island of Crete.

5 Which god was the father of Romulus and Remus?

6 What is the tradditional occupation of a leprachaun?

7 Which Greek hero killed the minotaur?

8 Who turned into a flower after spurning the love of Echo?

9 Which great hunter became a heavenly constellation after being slain by Artemis?

10 What is the name of the Roman counterpart of Zeus?

ANSWERS

1. Achilles 2. January (after Janus) 3. Perseus 4. Daedalus 5. Mars
6. Cobbler 7. Theseus 8. Narcissus 9. Orion 10. Jupiter

QUIZ 196

. . . .

1. At which sport did Jane Sixsmith represent England?

2. Who was nickamed The King and The Pelvis?

3. Who split from her husband Bruce Willis in 1998?

4. Who wrote the lyrics to the song 'Candle In The Wind'?

5. Which country was Celine Dion representing when she won the Eurovision Song Contest?

6. Which former US president is descended from a family of peanut farmers?

7. In which city did Muhammed Ali light the Olympic flame?

8. Who is the patron saint of mountaineers?

9. Who kept goal for England when they won the World Cup in 1966?

10. Which world champion did Robin Givens divorce in 1989?

ANSWERS

1. Field hockey 2. Elvis Presley 3. Demi Moore 4. Bernie Taupin
5. Switzerland 6. Jimmy Carter 7. Atlanta 8. St Bernard 9. Gordon Banks
10. Mike Tyson

QUIZ 197

• •

1 What is Frodo's last name in *The Lord Of The Rings*?

2 Which gospel writer wrote the first book of the New Testament?

3 Which black-and-orange striped feline features in the *Winnie the Pooh* tales?

4 How old was Noddy in 1999?

5 Is Billy Bunter's middle name Gerald, Granville or George?

6 Anne Elliott is the heroine of which novel by Jane Austen?

7 What is the name of the Good Witch of the North in *The Wizard Of Oz*?

8 What was won by William Golding in 1983, by John Steinbeck in 1962 and Winston Churchill in 1953?

9 Which comic strip heroine married Dagwood Bumstead?

10 Which school's motto is "Never Tickle A Sleeping Dragon"?

ANSWERS

1. Baggins 2. Matthew 3. Tigger 4. 50 5. George 6. *Persuasion* 7. Glinda
8. The Nobel Prize for Literature 9. Blondie 10. Hogwarts

QUIZ 198

• •

1 Which monarch was nicknamed Old Rowley?

2 Who seized power in Libya in 1969?

3 What title was used by German emperors until 1917?

4 Which 1600s conspiracy was led by Robert Catesby?

5 Which monk is credited with inventing champagne?

6 Which Sioux native American chief was killed in 1877 after surrendering to US troops?

7 Which dictator declared war on Britain and France in June 1940?

8 Which first lady of the USA was born Elizabeth Ann Bloomer?

9 Who was executed in 1793 and was played on film 145 years later by Norma Shearer?

10 Which classical composer was nicknamed The Red Priest?

ANSWERS

1. Charles II 2. Colonel Gadaffi 3. Kaiser 4. Gunpowder Plot 5. Dom Perignon 6. Chief Crazy Horse 7. Benito Mussolini 8. Betty Ford 9. Marie Antoinette 10. Antonio Vivaldi

QUIZ 199

1 In which 2001 film did Julia Roberts play the kidnapped girlfriend of Brad Pitt?

2 What was the last Bond film in which Lois Maxwell played Miss Moneypenny?

3 Which Swedish actress was the second wife of Peter Sellers?

4 Which 1994 film saw John Travolta dancing with Uma Thurman?

5 In the film *Gregory's Girl*, what sport did Gregory's girl play?

6 Who played the role of Sharkey in the 1981 film *Sharkey's Machine*?

7 Which 1967 film featured a chimpanzee called Cornelius?

8 Who on film sang 'Diamonds Are A Girls Best Friend' with Marilyn Monroe?

9 In which blockbuster movie did Jon Voight play President Franklin D Roosevelt?

10 Which giant ape was discovered living on Skull Island?

ANSWERS

1. *The Mexican* 2. *A View To A Kill* 3. Britt Ekland 4. *Pulp Fiction* 5. Football
6. Burt Reynolds 7. *The Planet Of The Apes* 8. Jane Russell 9. *Pearl Harbor*
10. King Kong

QUIZ 200

Who won a Best Actor Oscar for his role as…

1 Frank Slade in *Scent Of A Woman*?

2 Terry Malloy in *On The Waterfront*?

3 Kid Shelleen in *Cat Ballou*?

4 Wladyslaw Szpilman in *The Pianist*?

5 Howard Beale in *Network*?

6 Melvin Udall in *As Good As It Gets*?

7 Mac Sledge in *Tender Mercies*?

8 Ben Hur in *Ben Hur*?

9 Raymond Babbitt in *Rain Man*?

10 Lester Burnham in *American Beauty*?

ANSWERS

1. Al Pacino 2. Marlon Brando 3. Lee Marvin 4. Adrien Brody 5. Peter Finch
6. Jack Nicholson 7. Robert Duvall 8. Charlton Heston 9. Dustin Hoffman
10. Kevin Spacey

QUIZ 201

• •

1 For which crime was Sophia Loren jailed in 1982?

2 Which star of the film *Chaplin* received a jail sentence for drugs charges?

3 Why did Zsa Zsa Gabor serve three days in jail in 1988?

4 Which star of the TV series Mike Hammer was arrested in possession of cocaine at Heathrow airport?

5 Which pop star was arrested in a Beverly Hills park on April 7, 1998?

6 Which member of The Doors was the first rock star to be arrested on stage?

7 Which star of the film *48 Hours*, was arrested in 2002 for driving under the influence?

8 Which member of the female rock band Hole, was arrested aboard a plane for an air rage assault?

9 Which footballer penned a book entitled *Addicted* after serving a jail sentence for drink driving?

10 Which star of the film *Edward Scissorhands* received three years probation for shop lifting offences in 2002?

ANSWERS

1. Income tax evasion 2. Robert Downey Jnr 3. For assaulting a police officer 4. Stacey Keach 5. George Michael 6. Jim Morrison 7. Nick Nolte 8. Courtney Love 9. Tony Adams 10. Winona Ryder

QUIZ 202

1 At the Battle of Gettysburg, which general led the army of Northern Virginia?

2 Which country did Eric the Eel represent at the 2000 Sydney Olympics?

3 Which organization was founded by George Williams and immortalized in song by The Village People?

4 At which sport has Rachel Heyhoe-Flint captained England?

5 Which work by Vincent Van Gogh sold for almost £25 million at an auction in March 1987?

6 Which former US president was born Leslie Lynch King Jnr in 1917?

7 How many Best Actress Oscars did Katharine Hepburn win?

8 In which country did Gilbert and Sullivan set their opera *The Mikado*?

9 Was the horror movie star Boris Karloff born in Great Britain, the USA or Romania?

10 How many humans were aboard Noah's Ark?

ANSWERS

1. General Lee 2. Equatorial Guinea 3. YMCA 4. Cricket 5. *Sunflowers*
6. Gerald Ford 7. Four 8. Japan 9. Great Britain 10. Eight

QUIZ 203

• •

1 Which twin brothers accompanied the cartoon character Tin Tin?

2 What type of fish shares its name with Bob the Builder's pet cat?

3 Who has played Alf Garnett on TV for many years?

4 From which South American country did Paddington Bear travel to Britain?

5 What is the first name of Hopkirk in *Randall And Hopkirk Deceased*?

6 In which comedy series did Nerys Hughes play the role of Sandra Hutchinson?

7 Which wild west hero was played in the early days of television by William Boyd?

8 Which TV personality is associated with the catchphrase "Hello possums"?

9 Who played the title role in the TV detective series *Spender*?

10 Who performed the famed Monty Python 'parrot sketch' with John Cleese?

ANSWERS

1. The Thompson Twins 2. Pilchard 3. Warren Mitchell 4. Peru 5. Marty
6. *The Liver Birds* 7. Hopalong Cassidy 8. Dame Edna Everage 9. Jimmy Nail
10. Michael Palin

QUIZ 204

1 What does the O stand for in the name of the TV detective Harry O?

2 Which of the McGann brothers played the *Monicled Mutineer* on TV?

3 In which series, set in a POW camp, did Stephanie Cole play Dr Beatrice Mason?

4 Who plays the role of Henry Crabbe in *Pie In The Sky*?

5 Which Oscar winner played the role of Elizabeth I in the award-winning TV drama *Elizabeth R*?

6 Which of Charlie's Angels was portrayed by Kate Jackson?

7 Which children's puppet series featured the characters of Mike Mercury, Dr Beaker and Mitch the monkey?

8 Which husband and wife connect the comedy series *Chef* and *The Vicar of Dibley*?

9 Which cartoon family live in Orbit City with their pet dog Astro?

10 Who drove the Turbo Terrific in *Wacky Races*?

ANSWERS

1. Orwell 2. Paul McGann 3. *Tenko* 4. Richard Griffiths 5. Glenda Jackson
6. Sabrina Duncan 7. Supercar 8. Lenny Henry and Dawn French 9. The
Jetsons 10. Peter Perfect

QUIZ 205

. . . .

1   What did Medusa the gorgon have instead of hair?

2   Which horse sprang from the body of Medusa following her death?

3   Who killed Achilles with a fatal shot to his heel?

4   Who is the sister of Castor and Pollux?

5   In Greek mythology, who opened a box that released all the evils into the world?

6   Which mythological monsters possessed the heads of women and the bodies of birds?

7   Which Greek mythological figure killed his father and married his mother?

8   Which mountain is the home of the Greek gods?

9   Which founder of Carthage shares a four-letter name with a 21st-century pop star?

10 Who is the Greek god of the woods?

ANSWERS

1. Snakes 2. Pegasus 3. Paris 4. Helen of Troy 5. Pandora 6. Harpies
7. Oedipus 8. Mount Olympus 9. Dido 10. Pan

QUIZ 206

1 On whose life was the short-lived musical *Winnie* based?

2 By what six-letter name is John Clayton III better known?

3 Which Welshman was crowned World Snooker Champion in 1979?

4 Which Scotsman was crowned Formula One World Champion for the first time in 1969?

5 What connects Holly in the TV series *Red Dwarf* with Hal in the film *2001 A Space Odyssey*?

6 Who designed London's Marble Arch?

7 Which superhero owns a car called *Black Beauty*, driven by a chauffeur called Kato?

8 What colour is cartoon hero Tin Tin's dog?

9 Who was the vice president of George Bush Snr?

10 Who did George W Bush appoint as his vice president?

ANSWERS

1. Winston Churchill 2. Tarzan 3. Terry Griffiths 4. Jackie Stewart 5. Both are the names of computers 6. John Nash 7. The Green Hornet 8. White 9. Dan Quayle 10. Dick Cheney

QUIZ 207

. . . .

1 On which vessel was Jim Hawkins the cabin boy in *Treasure Island*?

2 Who created the literary villain Fu Manchu?

3 Which PG Wodehouse character is a member of the Drones Club and lives at Totleigh Towers?

4 Who wrote the play *The Caretaker*?

5 Under which name did brothers Jakob and Wilhelm write numerous fairytales?

6 Which town's rodent problem was solved by the Pied Piper?

7 Under what name did David John Moore Cornwell write several best-selling novels?

8 How are the Neil Simon creations of Felix Unger and Oscar Madison collectively known?

9 In which century did Edgar Allan Poe live?

10 How many men did the nursery rhyme character the Grand Old Duke Of York have under his command?

ANSWERS

1. *Hispaniola* 2. Sax Rohmer 3. Bertie Wooster 4. Harold Pinter 5. The Brothers Grimm 6. Hamelin 7. John Le Carré 8. The Odd Couple 9. 19th century 10. 10,000

QUIZ 208

1. In which country was Christopher Columbus born?

2. Which Roman emperor designed the Pantheon in Rome?

3. Who is the only English king to be crowned on a battlefield?

4. Name any year in which Dwight Eisenhower was president of the USA.

5. Who was president of the USA during World War I?

6. Who was Archbishop of Canterbury throughout the 1980s?

7. How many kings ruled Britain in the 20th century?

8. Robert Menzies is a past prime minister of which country?

9. Who founded the Methodist religion in the 18th century?

10. On which hill did King Harold lose the Battle of Hastings?

ANSWERS

1. Italy 2. Hadrian 3. Henry VII 4. 1953 - 1961 5. Woodrow Wilson 6. Robert Runcie 7. Four 8. Australia 9. John Wesley 10. Senlac Hill

QUIZ 209

• •

1 Who played the Boston Strangler in the 1968 film?

2 In which film did Catherine Zeta Douglas play the role of Velma Kelley?

3 Which pop hero was portrayed by Lou Diamond Phillips in the film *La Bamba*?

4 In which 1990 film did Kathy Bates play a disturbed retired nurse called Annie Wilkes?

5 Which school friend of Harry Potter is played on film by Emma Watson?

6 In which 2001 film did Denzel Washington play a crooked cop called Alonzo Harris?

7 Anne Bancroft seduced Dustin Hoffman in which film?

8 Which star of the film *The Magnificent Seven* was born Taidje Khan Jnr?

9 Emperor Zurg is the archenemy of which film hero?

10 Who played the title roles in the 1990s movies *The Wedding Singer* and *Big Daddy*?

ANSWERS

1. Tony Curtis 2. *Chicago* 3. Ritchie Valens 4. *Misery* 5. Hermione Granger
6. *Training Day* 7. *The Graduate* 8. Yul Brynner 9. Buzz Lightyear 10. Adam
Sandler

QUIZ 210

• •

Who played the leading lady of …

1 Clint Eastwood in *The Bridges Of Madison County*?

2 Humphrey Bogart in *Casablanca*?

3 Ben Affleck in *Pearl Harbor*?

4 John Wayne in *The Quiet Man*?

5 Jon Voight in *The Champ*?

6 Mel Gibson in *Bird On A Wire*?

7 Jack Nicholson in *The Shining*?

8 Arnold Schwarzenegger in *True Lies*?

9 Harrison Ford in *Witness*?

10 Errol Flynn in *The Adventures Of Robin Hood*?

ANSWERS

1. Meryl Streep 2. Ingrid Bergman 3. Kate Beckinsale 4. Maureen O'Hara
5. Faye Dunaway 6. Goldie Hawn 7. Shelley Duvall 8. Jamie Lee Curtis
9. Kelly McGillis 10. Olivia de Havilland

QUIZ 211

• •

1 How did Mehmet Ali Agca gain notoriety in 1981?

2 Which Mafia boss acquired the nickname of Teflon Don?

3 Which Oscar-winning actor played a sadistic criminal called Big Boy Caprice in the 1990 film *Dick Tracy*?

4 Which femal gangster was portrayed by Shelley Winters in the film *Bloody Mama*?

5 Who was shot dead in July 1934 in front of the Biograph Theatre?

6 What first name was shared by the body snatchers Burke and Hare?

7 Which Dickens novel featured a grave robber called Jerry Cruncher?

8 In which 2002 film did Robin Williams play a stalker called Seymour Parrish?

9 In 1999, which 87-year-old British grandmother was exposed as a Russian spy?

10 In which 1990 film did Joe Pesci play a gangster called Tommy De Vito?

ANSWERS

1. He attempted to assassinate the Pope 2. John Gotti 3. Al Pacino 4. Ma Barker 5. John Dillinger 6. William 7. *A Tale Of Two Cities* 8. *One Hour Photo* 9. Melita Norwood 10. *Goodfellas*

QUIZ 212

1 Who helped to popularize line dancing with his 1992 hit 'Achy Breaky Heart'?

2 Who was struck blind for sneaking a look at Lady Godiva?

3 Which composer of the *Pink Panther* theme died in 1994?

4 What is the nationality of the inventor James Watt?

5 In which sport did Britain's Karen Pickering become a world champion?

6 Who shared the Nobel Peace Prize with FW De Klerk in 1993?

7 By what name is the hip-swivelling pop hero, born Thomas Woodward, better known?

8 Who composed the opera *The Flying Dutchman*?

9 Who was elected prime minister of Great Britain in 1976?

10 When Robert Redford played the Sundance Kid who played Butch Cassidy?

ANSWERS

1. Billy Ray Cyrus 2. Peeping Tom 3. Henry Mancini 4. Scottish
5. Swimming 6. Nelson Mandela 7. Tom Jones 8. Richard Wagner 9. James Callaghan 10. Paul Newman

QUIZ 213

1 Which U.N.C.L.E. agent holds badge number 11?

2 In which series did Lee Majors play the role of Colt Seavers?

3 What is the name of Dick Dastardly's canine companion?

4 Which army major was found guilty of cheating on the TV game show *Who Wants To Be A Millionaire*?

5 Which literary and TV barrister lives at 25B, Foxbury Court, Gloucester Rd, London?

6 What was the name of the cross-eyed lion in Daktari?

7 In which year did Dr Who make his TV debut?

8 Who played Howard Cunnigham in *Happy Days* and Frank Dowling in *Father Dowling Investigates*?

9 In which Emmy Award-winning series did Burt Reynolds play the character of Wood Newton?

10 What is the name of Noggin the Nog's evil uncle?

ANSWERS

1. Napoleon Solo 2. *The Fall Guy* 3. Muttley 4. Charles Ingram
5. *Rumpole of the Bailey* 6. Clarence 7. 1963 8. Tom Bosley 9. *Evening Shade*
10. Nogbad the Bad

QUIZ 214

. . . .

1 Which comedy series featured a married couple called Rene and Edith Artois?

2 Which actor left the Tardis for Scatterbrook Farm?

3 Which children's favourites live at Home Hill?

4 Which writer links the TV shows *Bread*, *Butterflies* and *Solo*?

5 What kind of animal is the cartoon hero Quick Draw McGraw?

6 Which singer, born Mary O'Brien, sang the first song in the very first edition of *Top Of The Pops* in 1964?

7 Who played the role of Jed Clampett in the US sitcom *The Beverly Hillbillies*?

8 Which star of *Last Of The Summer Wine* penned an autobiography entitled *Wrinkles And All*?

9 What is the name of the burger-munching compatriot of *Popeye the Sailorman*?

10 How many children were in *The Partridge Family*?

ANSWERS

1. *Allo Allo* 2. Jon Pertwee 3. *The Teletubbies* 4. Carla Lane 5. Horse
6. Dusty Springfield 7. Buddy Ebsen 8. Kathy Staff 9. Wimpy 10. Five

QUIZ 215

1 Which female cartoon character was banned on the grounds of immorality in the 1930s?

2 What is the name of the newspaper read by Fred Flintstone?

3 Who captained the sailing vessel the *Black Pig*?

4 Which animated superhero's secret headquarters is located in a postbox on Baker Street?

5 What is the name of the hypnotic snake in *The Jungle Book*?

6 Jafar is the foe of which Disney animated hero?

7 Which gang assisted Penelope Pitstop in *The Adventures Of Penelope Pitstop*?

8 Which Warner Brothers animated hero was the first cartoon character to feature on a US postage stamp?

9 Which animated insect sang 'When You Wish Upon A Star' in Disney's *Pinocchio*?

10 What type of fish is Nemo in the film *Finding Nemo*?

ANSWERS

1. Betty Boop 2. *Daily Slate* 3. Captain Pugwash 4. Dangermouse 5. Kaa
6. Aladdin 7. The Ant Hill Mob 8. Bugs Bunny 9. Jiminy Cricket 10 A clown fish

QUIZ 216

. . . .

1 Which of the seven dwarfs has the shortest name?

2 Which of the seven dwarfs has the longest name?

3 Who was the oldest member of the Spice Girls?

4 Who was the first triple jumper to clear a distance of over 18 metres?

5 Which sign of the zodiac is represented by Castor and Pollux?

6 Who scored the majority of England's goals in the 1986 World Cup soccer finals?

7 Which religious post was taken up by David Michael Hope in 1995?

8 In which sport has Victor Barna won several world titles?

9 In Arthurian legend, who threw Excalibur into the lake?

10 In which sport has Tim Foster won Olympic gold for Great Britain?

ANSWERS

1.Doc 2.Bashful 3.Geri Halliwell 4.Jonathan Edwards 5.Gemini 6.Gary Lineker 7.Archbishop of York 8.Table tennis 9.Sir Bevedere 10.Rowing

QUIZ 217

• •

1 Which Dickens novel features the cruel character of Wackford Squeers?

2 Who was the first ever poet laureate?

3 Which nursery rhyme character cried through the locks, dressed in his nightgown?

4 Who created Billy Bunter?

5 Which Shakespeare play features the character of Claudius, the King of Denmark?

6 The book *The Other Side Of The Rainbow* chronicles the turbulent life story of which movie icon?

7 Who created the fictional diarist Bridget Jones?

8 Who penned the controversial novel *A Clockwork Orange*?

9 Who directed the equally controversial film adaptation of the novel *A Clockwork Orange*?

10 Which former England cricket captain has written a novel entitled *Deep Cover*?

ANSWERS

1. *Nicholas Nickleby* 2. John Dryden 3. Wee Willie Winkie 4. Frank Richards 5. *Hamlet* 6. Judy Garland 7. Helen Fielding 8. Anthony Burgess 9. Stanley Kubrick 10. Ian Botham

QUIZ 218

1 Which biblical character sold his birthright for a mess of potage?

2 Who captained HMS *Victory* at the Battle of Trafalgar?

3 Who was British prime minister from 1970 to 1974?

4 Which daughter of Cepheus was rescued from the clutches of a sea monster by the Greek hero Perseus?

5 Which king of France became known as The Citizen King?

6 Who painted *The Potato Eaters*?

7 What nickname was given to the English king Ethelred II?

8 To whom was Queen Victoria referring when she said "He speaks to me as if I were a public meeting"?

9 What was the name of Captain James Cook's flagship during his voyage to Antarctica?

10 Was Calamity Jane's real first name Mary, Martha or Meg?

ANSWERS

1. Esau 2. Captain Hardy 3. Edward Heath 4. Andromeda 5. Louis-Philippe
6. Vincent Van Gogh 7. The Unready 8. William Gladstone 9. *Resolution*
10. Martha

QUIZ 219

- -

1   Which film features the characters of Alexandra Medford, Sukie Ridgemont and Jane Spofford?

2   Who played the serial killer in the 1995 crime thriller *Seven*?

3   In which 2002 futuristic thriller did Tom Cruise play the role of Detective John Anderton?

4   Which actor has played Lee Harvey Oswald, Count Dracula and Sid Vicious on the big screen?

5   Which veteran movie star won an Oscar for his portrayal of Curly in the film *City Slickers*?

6   Who directed the 1962 movie epic *Lawrence Of Arabia*?

7   What is the name of the actor brother of Charlie Sheen?

8   In which 2002 film did Meryl Streep play the role of Clarissa Vaughan?

9   Who played Roberta Waterbury in the 1970 film *The Railway Children*?

10 In which 2002 film did Mel Gibson play the role of Lieutenant Colonel Hal Moore?

ANSWERS

1. The Witches Of Eastwick 2. Kevin Spacey 3. *Minority Report* 4. Gary Oldman 5. Jack Palance 6. David Lean 7. Emilio Estevez 8. *The Hours* 9. Jenny Agutter 10. *We Were Soldiers*

QUIZ 220

• •

1   In the Bond movie *Licence To Kill*, 007 was the best man at whose wedding?

2   What was the occupation of Bruce Willis in the film *Armageddon*?

3   Who co-starred in 11 films with Richard Burton?

4   Who played the title role in *Kindergarten Cop*?

5   What is the home country of Dr Zhivago?

6   In which film did Robin Williams play a disc jockey in the US armed forces?

7   Which actor played the title roles in the films *Junior Bonner*, *Tom Horn* and *Nevada Smith*?

8   'We Don't Need Another Hero' is the theme song to which movie sequel?

9   Which member of a famous acting family links the films *Against All Odds*, *The Vanishing* and *Starman*?

10 Which film featured a dance floor hero called Tony Manero?

ANSWERS

1. Felix Leiter 2. Oil driller 3. Elizabeth Taylor 4. Arnold Schwarzenegger
5. Russia 6. *Good Morning Vietnam* 7. Steve McQueen 8. *Mad Max: Beyond Thunderdome* 9. Jeff Bridges 10. *Saturday Night Fever*

QUIZ 221

• •

1 In which century were the Salem witch trials held?

2 In which city was John F Kennedy assassinated?

3 Which personal secretary of Adolph Hitler was sentenced to death in his absence at the Nuremburg Trials?

4 Who played *The Birdman Of Alcatraz* in a 1962 film?

5 Which man of the cloth is a murder suspect in the game of Cluedo?

6 Which serial killer became known as The Whitechapel Monster?

7 Against whom did Paula Jones launch legal action in 1994?

8 In which film did Michael Caine play a killer called Dr Robert Elliot?

9 In which decade was Jesse James killed?

10 Which 1978 film told the true story of Billy Hayes and his time in a Turkish prison?

ANSWERS

1. 17th century 2. Dallas 3. Martin Borman 4. Burt Lancaster 5. Reverend Green 6. Jack The Ripper 7. Bill Clinton 8. *Dressed To Kill* 9. 1880s 10. *Midnight Express*

QUIZ 222

● ●

1   In *The Arabian Nights*, who is the heroic son of Mustafa the tailor?

2   Who recorded the albums *Tubular Bells* and *Hergest Ridge*?

3   In which country was Harry Houdini born?

4   Daddy Warbucks is the guardian of which orphan?

5   How are the superheroes Reed Richard, The Invisible Woman, The Human Torch and The Thing known?

6   In the 1960s Harold Holt served as prime minister of which country?

7   Which supermodel divorced Richard Gere in 1995?

8   In whivh year was Bobby Kennedy assassinated?

9   What was the name of Ronald Reagan's wife and first lady?

10 Which French football star was voted PFA Player of the Year in 1999?

ANSWERS

1. Aladdin 2. Mike Oldfield 3. Hungary 4. Little Orphan Annie 5. The Fantastic Four 6. Australia 7. Cindy Crawford 8. 1968 9. Nancy 10 David Ginola

QUIZ 223

1 In *Star Trek*, which is the home planet of Mr Spock's mother?

2 Who played the Bionic Woman on TV?

3 In 1975, who became Britain's first national female newsreader on TV?

4 What is the name of the aggressive nephew of Scooby Doo?

5 In which sitcom did Thora Hird play an undertaker called Ivy Unsworth?

6 Which actor plays the politician Alan Clark in a 2004 TV drama?

7 Kevin the gerbil is the best friend of which rodent hero?

8 Which superior of Inspector Jack Frost is portrayed on TV by Bruce Alexander?·

9 Which department store did Miss Brahms and Mrs Slocombe work for?

10 Captain Christopher Pike was the first captain of which vessel?

ANSWERS

1. Earth 2. Lindsay Wagner 3. Angela Rippon 4. Scrappy Doo 5. *In Loving Memory* 6. John Hurt 7. Roland Rat 8. Superintendent Mullet 9. *Grace Brothers* 10. USS *Enterprise*

QUIZ 224

....

Unravel the anagrams to give the names of ten
    cartoon characters.

1   FUR MEDDLE

2   GANGS PULSES

3   A MOB SPRINTS

4   LANK DUD COD

5   SLYER VETS

6   URN ADORNER

7   DUTY GAWPED

8   HUGE MISTY MO

9   CHEAT LET FIX

10 PETITE YEW

ANSWERS

QUIZ 225

• •

1 Which aviator acquired the nickname of the Lone Eagle?

2 Which serial killer became known as The Son of Sam?

3 Which 4th-century warrior was known as The Scourge of God?

4 Which West Indian fast bowler is nicknamed Big Bird?

5 Which Russian tsar was known as The Terrible?

6 Which baseball legend was nicknamed The Yankee Clipper?

7 Which Italian soccer star was nicknamed The Divine Ponytail?

8 Which English ruler was known as Ironside?

9 Silent Cal was the nickname of which US president?

10 Which former British prime minister was known as The Welsh Wizard?

ANSWERS

1. Charles Lindbergh 2. David Berkowitz 3. Atilla the Hun 4. Joel Garner
5. Ivan 6. Joe di Maggio 7. Roberto di Baggio 8. Edmund II 9. Calvin
Coolidge 10. David Lloyd George

QUIZ 226

- -

1 Who is the patron saint of fishermen?

2 What was the first name of Barnum of Barnum and Bailey's Circus?

3 Which African president was assassinated in 1981 while attending a military parade?

4 Which Beatle regretted saying "We're more popular than Jesus now"?

5 Which Greek god is the father of Perseus?

6 Which city in the USA is home to JFK Airport?

7 Who founded Virgin Records in 1969?

8 In which country was former England cricket captain Nasser Hussain born?

9 In which river was Jesus baptized by John the Baptist?

10 Who won an Oscar for his portrayal of Gandhi?

ANSWERS

1. St Peter 2. Phineus 3. Anwar Sadat 4. John Lennon 5. Zeus 6. New York
7. Richard Branson 8. India 9. River Jordan 10. Ben Kingsley

QUIZ 227

• •

Unravel the anagrams to give the names of ten literary
    characters.

1 VIOLET WRITS

2 A PERRY TROTH

3 HOE TOLL

4 MENDS A JOB

5 WHISK JAM IN

6 NEAT PREP

7 LACED LINER

8 FAUN CHUM

9 STEAMY ROW

10 BRAT BRIBER

ANSWERS

1. Oliver Twist 2. Harry Potter 3. Othello 4. James Bond 5. Jim Hawkins
6. Peter Pan 7. Cinderella 8. Fu Manchu 9. Tom Sawyer 10. Brer Rabbit

QUIZ 228

. . . .

1 In which city was Joan of Arc burnt at the stake?

2 Who was the first man to reach the South Pole?

3 Which duo made the first nonstop flight across the Atlantic Ocean in 1919?

4 Who is the Greek god of the sea?

5 Did Alexander the Great die before Jesus Christ or after?

6 Which Cuban leader was excommunicated in 1962?

7 Who was Hitler's propaganda chief?

8 In 1964, Hastings Banda became the leader of which African country?

9 In America's old west who was known as Little Miss Sure Shot?

10 Who was shot dead on November 24, 1963, two days after being arrested?

ANSWERS

1. Rouen 2. Roald Amundsen 3. Alcock and Brown 4. Poseidon 5. Before (323BC) 6. Fidel Castro 7. Josef Goebbels 8. Malawi 9. Annie Oakley 10. Lee Harvey Oswald

QUIZ 229

1 Who played the villain of the piece in the films *The Man With The Golden Gun* and *The Wicker Man*?

2 Who was 45 years old when he first played James Bond on film?

3 Which film star was nicknamed Hollywood's Mermaid?

4 Which star of *The Great Escape* was born Charles Buchinski?

5 Which actor commits the murders in the movie classic *Kind Hearts And Coronets*?

6 Which movie icon, born Jane Peters, perished in a plane crash in 1942?

7 In which film did Dennis Hopper play a manic villain known as The Deacon?

8 In which classic British movie did Michael Caine play Charlie Croker?

9 Who played Ted Kramer in *Kramer Vs Kramer*?

10 Who played Joanna Kramer in *Kramer Vs Kramer*?

ANSWERS

1. Christopher Lee 2. Roger Moore 3. Esther Williams 4. Charles Bronson
5. Dennis Price 6. Carole Lombard 7. *Waterworld* 8. *The Italian Job*
9. Dustin Hoffman 10. Meryl Streep

QUIZ 230

. . . .

1 Which film character delivered the famous line "Frankly my dear, I don't give a damn"?

2 In which film did John Travolta play Vincent Vega?

3 What type of vehicle did Robert De Niro drive when playing the film character Travis Bickle?

4 Who played the title role in the 1996 film *Michael Collins*?

5 Which character was played by Bert Kwouk in *The Pink Panther* movies?

6 Which actor played Dr Loomis in *Halloween* and Himmler in *The Eagle Has Landed*?

7 What is the name of the sherrif portrayed by John Wayne in *True Grit*?

8 Which spy was portrayed by Michael Caine in *The Ipcress File*?

9 Who played Liberty Valence in the film *The Man Who Shot Liberty Valence*?

10 Which film hero transformed into the film villain Darth Vader?

ANSWERS

1. Rhett Butler in *Gone With The Wind* 2. *Pulp Fiction* 3. Taxi in *Taxi Driver*
4. Liam Neeson 5. Cato 6. Donald Pleasence 7. Rooster Cogburn 8. Harry Palmer 9. Lee Marvin 10. Anakin Skywalker

QUIZ 231

. . . .

1   Who replaced Johnny Torrio as the leader of the Chicago Mafia?

2   Which murder suspect in Cluedo shares his name with a condiment?

3   What did the F stand for in the name of the convict Robert F Stroud?

4   What was the name of Dick Turpin's faithful steed?

5   What was the last name of the Great Train Robber Buster, as played on film by Phil Collins?

6   No Name Maddox was an alias used by which notorious criminal?

7   What was used to behead Anne Boleyn?

8   In which 1991 film did Bruce Willis play a cat burglar?

9   Which murderer was himself murdered in Walpole Prison in 1973?

10 In 1594 Dr Lopez was executed for an alleged assassination attempt against which monarch?

ANSWERS

1. Al Capone 2. Colonel Mustard 3. Franklin 4. Black Bess 5. Edwards
6. Charles Manson 7. A sword 8. *Hudson Hawk* 9. Albert De Salvo, or The
Boston Strangler 10. Elizabeth I

QUIZ 232

• •

1 Who officially opened the 1936 Olympic Games?

2 Which golfer ran a business called The Great White Shark Company?

3 In what decade did Matthew Webb become the first person to swim the English Channel?

4 Which European country's red-and-white striped flag represents the tunic of Duke Leopold V?

5 In which year was Lady Diana killed in a Paris car crash?

6 Which planet is named after the Roman messenger of the gods?

7 In 1981, Jerry Rawlings became leader of which African country?

8 Who was the only Irish boxer to hold a world title in the 1980s?

9 In the Bible who is the elder brother of Moses?

10 Who was elected president of South Africa in 1994?

ANSWERS

1. Adolf Hitler 2. Greg Norman 3. 1870s 4. Austria 5. 1997 6. Mercury
7. Ghana 8. Barry McGuigan 9. Aaron 10. Nelson Mandela

QUIZ 233

● ●

1 What is the first name of Steed in *The Avengers*?

2 Who is the only female contestant in *Wacky Races*?

3 What is the last name of Joey in the US comedy series *Friends*?

4 Which detective duo created by Reginald Hill are played on TV by Warren Clarke and Colin Buchanan?

5 What musical instrument does Zoot play in *The Muppet Show*?

6 Which programme features the characters of Melody, Rhapsody, Symphony, Harmony and Destiny?

7 According to the TV theme who are "creepy and kookie and altogether ooky"?

8 Which bad-mannered canine accompanied Bob Carolgees?

9 Professor Mariner was the father of which aquatic cartoon hero?

10 TV presenter Jerry Springer was formerly a mayor of which US city?

ANSWERS

1. John 2. Penelope Pitstop 3. Tribbiani 4. Dalziel And Pascoe 5. Saxophone
6. *Captain Scarlet* 7. The Addams Family 8. Spit the Dog 9. Marine Boy
10. Cincinnati

QUIZ 234

• •

1 What colour is the Trotter's three-wheeler van in *Only Fools And Horses*?

2 Which TV duo speak their own language, known as 'oddle poddle'?

3 What type of creature is Idris in *Ivor The Engine*?

4 On *The Muppet Show* who is the reluctant assistant of Dr Bunsen Honeydew?

5 In which series did Judi Bowker play the role of Victoria Gordon?

6 What is Chippy Minton's job in *Camberwick Green*?

7 Which park is the home of Yogi Bear and Boo Boo?

8 Who is Bodie's partner in *The Professionals*?

9 In which century was the 1960s series of *Star Trek* set?

10 What is Lady Penelope's surname in *Thunderbirds*?

ANSWERS

1. Yellow 2. Bill and Ben 3. Dragon 4. Beaker 5. *The Adventures of Black Beauty* 6. Carpenter 7. Jellystone Park 8. Doyle 9. 23rd 10. Creighton-Ward

QUIZ 235

Use the initials to solve the nicknames of the following famous people.

1	William Gladstone	The GOM
2	Robert F Stroud	The B of A
3	Paavo Nurmi	The FF
4	Stanley Matthews	The W of D
5	Anne of Cleves	The FM
6	Lana Turner	The SG
7	Robert Burns	The B of A
8	Joan of Arc	The M of O
9	Benny Goodman	The K of S
10	Joseph Holson Jagger	The MWB the B at MC

ANSWERS

1. The Grand Old Man 2. The Birdman of Alcatraz 3. The Flying Finn 4. The Wizard of Dribble 5. The Flanders Mare 6. The Sweater Girl 7. The Bard of Ayrshire 8. The Maid of Orleans 9. The King of Swing 10. The Man Who Broke The Bank At Monte Carlo

QUIZ 236

. . . .

1 Who was the wife of King Arthur?

2 Who made a famed speech in 1963 that began with the words "I have a dream"?

3 Which comedian who lived past the age of 100, was born Nathan Birnbaum?

4 What was the title of the first hit record for The Spice Girls?

5 Who was the first member of The Beatles to have a solo No 1 hit?

6 Who said "Give me a lever long enough and I will move the world"?

7 Who wrote the musical *Copacabana*?

8 What is the Roman god Jupiter's wife's name?

9 Who replaced Neil Kinnock as leader of the Labour Party?

10 Which European country's flag was inspired by the coat of arms of William of Orange?

ANSWERS

1. Guinevere 2. Martin Luther King 3. George Burns 4. 'Wannabee'
5. George Harrison 6. Archimedes 7. Barry Manilow 8. Juno 9. John Smith
10. The Netherlands

QUIZ 237

. . . .

1 What was the first name of the poet Lord Byron?

2 Who married Anne Hathaway in 1582?

3 Who created the literary hero Professor Challenger?

4 What does the J stand for in the name of *Peter Pan* author JM Barrie?

5 Winston Smith is the hero of which George Orwell novel?

6 What T is the name of a clown in *As You Like It*?

7 Miss Lemon is the secretary of which literary sleuth?

8 Who wrote the novel *The Call Of The Wild*?

9 Which resident of Wonderland owned a piece of headgear bearing a price tag of 10/6d?

10 Which seafaring novel is narrated by Ishmael?

ANSWERS

1. George 2. William Shakespeare 3. Arthur Conan Doyle 4. James 5. *1984*
6. Touchstone 7. Hercule Poirot 8. Jack London 9. The Mad Hatter
10. *Moby Dick*

QUIZ 238

• •

1 Was George Washington's wife called Martha, Mary or Melissa?

2 In 1926 which first was achieved by Gertrude Ederle in a time of 14 hours and 39 minutes?

3 Which part of Adam's body was used to make Eve?

4 In British history who acquired the nickname Bloody Mary?

5 Which song was rearranged by Elton John and Bernie Taupin on the death of Princess Diana?

6 King Idris was the last monarch of which African country?

7 How many of Henry VIII wives were beheaded?

8 Who was the first US president to live in the White House?

9 Which woman was prime minister of Israel from 1969 to 1974?

10 Which monarch was known as The Wisest Fool In Christendom?

ANSWERS

1. Martha 2. First woman to swim the Channel 3. Rib 4. Mary Tudor
5. *Candle In The Wind* 6. Libya 7. Two 8. John Adams 9. Golda Meir
10. James I

QUIZ 239

• •

In which film did Clint Eastwood play…

1 A retired astronaut called Frank Corvin?

2 A gold prospector called Sylvester Newel?

3 A big game hunter called John Wilson?

4 A DJ called Dave Carver?

5 A thief called Luther Whitney?

6 A convict called Frank Morris?

7 A deputy sheriff called Walt Coogan?

8 A retired gunslinger called William Munny?

9 A jet pilot called Mitchell Gant?

10 A bare knuckle fighter called Philo Beddoe?

ANSWERS

1. *Space Cowboys* 2. *Paint Your Wagon* 3. *White Hunter Black Heart* 4. *Play Misty For Me* 5. *Absolute Power* 6. *Escape From Alcatraz* 7. *Coogan's Bluff* 8. *Unforgiven* 9. *Firefox* 10. *Every Which Way But Loose* or *Any Which Way You Can*

QUIZ 240

● ●

1 In which film did Marilyn Monroe play the role of Sugar Kane?

2 Which detective was played by Elliot Gould in the film *The Long Goodbye*?

3 Who played Lara in the 1965 movie epic *Dr Zhivago*?

4 In which movie western did Dean Martin play the brother of John Wayne?

5 Who played the role of Mr Bumble in the Oscar winning musical *Oliver*?

6 Judge Doom is the villain of the piece in which 1988 film?

7 In which 1996 film did Brad Pitt play a terrorist called Frankie Maguire?

8 Who has been played on film by Boris Karloff, Kenneth Branagh, Peter Cushing and Sting?

9 In which 1998 film did Judi Dench play Elizabeth I?

10 Who did Gene Kelly play in the 1948 version of *The Three Musketeers*?

ANSWERS

1. *Some Like It Hot* 2. Philip Marlowe 3. Julie Christie 4. *The Sons Of Katie Elder* 5. Harry Secombe 6. *Who Framed Roger Rabbit* 7. *Devil's Own* 8. Baron Frankenstein 9. *Shakespeare In Love* 10. D'Artagnan

QUIZ 241

• •

Who played the following villains in the given films?

1 1960 Norman Bates in *Psycho*
2 1980 Emperor Ming in *Flash Gordon*
3 1991 Max Cady in *Cape Fear*
4 1986 Hannibal Lecter in *Manhunter*
5 1991 Hannibal Lecter in *Silence Of The Lambs*
6 1997 Mr Freeze in *Batman And Robin*
7 1995 Two Face in *Batman Forever*
8 1987 Alex Forrest in *Fatal Attraction*
9 1984 Freddy Krueger in *Nightmare On Elm Street*
10 2003 Bullseye in *Daredevil*

ANSWERS

1. Anthony Perkins 2. Max Von Sydow 3. Robert De Niro 4. Brian Cox
5. Anthony Hopkins 6. Arnold Schwarzenegger 7. Tommy Lee Jones
8. Glenn Close 9. Robert Englund 10. Colin Farrell

QUIZ 242

• •

1   In which town did Superman live as a boy?

2   Which English footballer joined the Japanese club Grampus 8 in 1992?

3   What does the D stand for in the name of the US president, Dwight D Eisenhower?

4   In which country was Alfred Nobel born?

5   What is the nationality of Aladdin?

6   What is the signature tune of the Glenn Miller Band?

7   The video for which song saw Michael Jackson transformed into a zombie and a werewolf?

8   Who was sent off in the 1998 World Cup after kicking Diego Simeone?

9   What links the stage name of the pop star Orville Burrell with the cartoon series *Scooby Doo*?

10 What nickname was given to the flying ace Manfred Von Richtofen?

ANSWERS

1. Smallville 2. Gary Lineker 3. David 4. Sweden 5. Chinese 6. 'Moonlight Serenade' 7. 'Thriller' 8. David Beckham 9. Shaggy 10. The Red Baron

QUIZ 243

. . . .

1 Who pilots *Thunderbird 1*?

2 What is the home state of Deputy Dawg?

3 Which cardinal was portrayed by David Suchet in the 2003 TV drama *Henry VIII*?

4 Laura Holt was the sidekick of which TV hero?

5 Which actor played the role of Ralph Ernest Gorse in *The Charmer*?

6 What colour of coat is worn by the employees of Maplins Holiday Camp?

7 Which New York cop began sucking lollipops in a bid to stop smoking?

8 Which comedian voiced the space-age hero Captain Kremmen?

9 On which island did Tattoo and Mr Roarke welcome visitors?

10 Which actor connects the TV shows, *Forever Green, Upstairs Downstairs* and *Please Sir*?

ANSWERS

1. Scott Tracy 2. Mississippi 3. Thomas Wolsey 4. Remington Steele 5. Nigel Havers 6. Yellow 7. Kojak 8,. Kenny Everett 9. Fantasy Island 10. John Alderton

QUIZ 244

• •

1 What does the T stand for in the acronym TARDIS?

2 Which terrorist organization is the archenemy of the men from U.N.C.L.E.?

3 When Bill Bixby played Dr Banner, who played the Incredible Hulk?

4 Who was often seen sharing a bed with Ernie on *Sesame Street*?

5 What type of creature is Penfold in *Dangermouse*?

6 Who presented the nature series *The Botanic Man*?

7 What is the first name of the Bionic Woman?

8 What does Popeye have tattooed on his arm?

9 The Beverly Hillbillies lived in a suburb of which city?

10 Who owns the nuclear power station in *The Simpsons*?

ANSWERS

QUIZ 245

• •

Name any year in which the following people were
    alive:

1 Sir Humphrey Davy

2 HG Wells

3 Robert The Bruce

4 Ludwig Van Beethoven

5 Rembrandt

6 Genghis Khan

7 Napoleon Bonaparte

8 Robert Burns

9 Vincent Van Gogh

10 Edward Elgar

ANSWERS

1. 1778–1829 2. 1866–1946 3. 1274–1329 4. 1770–1827 5. 1606–1669
6. 1162–1227 7. 1769–1821 8. 1759–1796 9. 1853–1890 10. 1857–1934

QUIZ 246

. . . .

1 In which soap opera do Fred and Lily live at Lower Loxley Hall?

2 Which Oscar-winning actor was the subject of a 1984 hit record by Madness?

3 The Valkyries are the handmaidens of which Norse god?

4 In what year was Princess Anne born?

5 By what name is the operatic heroine Cio Cio San better known?

6 Which duo have had hits singing about Susie, Claudette, Jenny, Mary, Cathy and Lucille?

7 Who founded the Microsoft Corporation with Bill Gates?

8 Which godfather of soul was backed by the Famous Flames?

9 In which city did John Lennon and Yoko Ono stage their famed bed-in peace protest?

10 By what name is Kathy Kane known when donning a cape and mask?

ANSWERS

1. *The Archers* 2. Michael Caine 3. Odin 4. 1950 5. Madam Butterfly
6. The Everly Brothers 7. Paul G Allen 8. James Brown 9. Amsterdam
10. Batwoman

QUIZ 247

• •

1 In which county does Harry Potter live with his Uncle Vernon?

2 At what number of Baker Street does Sherlock Holmes live?

3 Philip Pirrup is the hero of which Dickens novel?

4 In Rudyard Kipling's *The Jungle Book* is Ikky a parrot, a panther or a porcupine?

5 In *Romeo And Juliet* who dies first: Romeo or Juliet?

6 How old was Adrian Mole when he began writing his first diary?

7 Who is the central character of Oscar Wilde's only novel?

8 Who is Shakespeare's Moor of Venice?

9 What is Snow White's coffin made from?

10 What is the name of the joey in the *Winnie the Pooh* tales?

ANSWERS

1. Surrey 2. 221b 3. *Great Expectations* 4. Porcupine 5. Romeo 6. 13 and three quarters 7. Dorian Grey 8. Othello 9. Glass 10. Roo

QUIZ 248

. . . .

1   In the duo of Gilbert and Sullivan, which one wrote the music?

2   What was Peter Conrad the third person to achieve?

3   Who married Aristotle Onassis in 1968?

4   Who designed London's Monument, to commemorate the Great Fire of London?

5   In which Spanish town was Pablo Picasso born?

6   Which World Cup hero wrote the book *1966 And All That*?

7   Which epic work by the Greek poet Homer is set in the 10th year of the Trojan War?

8   In 1913, the year of his death, who wrote in his diary, "Great God this is an awful place"?

9   Who said "I know I have the body of a weak and feeble woman, but I have the heart and stomach of a king"?

10 Which English monarch was known as The Lionheart?

ANSWERS

1. Sullivan 2. Set foot on the moon 3. Jackie Kennedy 4. Sir Christopher Wren 5. Malaga 6. Geoff Hurst 7. *The Iliad* 8. Captain Robert Falcon Scott 9. Queen Elizabeth I 10. Richard I

QUIZ 249

. . . .

1 Who played the role of Ted in *Bill And Ted's Excellent Adventure*?

2 Which martial arts expert links the films *Rush Hour*, *Shanghai Noon* and *Rumble In The Bronx*?

3 In which animated movie did Sylvester Stallone provide the voice of an insect called Weaver?

4 Who is the only person to have won more than 30 Oscars?

5 Who co-starred with Doris Day in the films *Pillow Talk* and *Lover Come Back*?

6 Who was portrayed by Denzel Washington in the film *Cry Freedom*?

7 Which Beatles song was also the title of their first film?

8 What does Colin Farrell findhimself trapped inside for the duration of a 2002 film?

9 Who played juror number eight in the 1957 film *Twelve Angry Men*?

10 What is the second *Harry Potter* novel to be filmed?

ANSWERS

1. Keanu Reeves 2. Jackie Chan 3. *Antz* 4. Walt Disney 5. Rock Hudson
6. Steve Beko 7.' A Hard Day's Night' 8. Phone booth 9. Henry Fonda
10. *Harry Potter And The Chamber Of Secrets*

QUIZ 250

1 What is the name of the rooster voiced by Mel Gibson in *Chicken Run*?

2 Which vampire-battling hero has been played on film by Peter Cushing, Anthony Hopkins and Mel Brooks?

3 Which song did Laurel & Hardy sing in the film *Way Out West*?

4 In which animated film did Angela Lansbury provide the voice of Mrs Potts?

5 What is Steve Martin's profession in the film comedy *Roxanne*?

6 Who played the role of Will in the film *Good Will Hunting*?

7 Which war hero did Charlton Heston portray in the film *Khartoum*?

8 Who played the role of Michael Corleone in three films?

9 In which film did Richard Gere say "I want to fly jets"?

10 What was Elvis Presley's first film?

ANSWERS

1. Rocky 2. Professor Van Helsing 3. 'The Trail Of The Lonesome Pine'
4. *Beauty And The Beast* 5. Fire Chief 6. Matt Damon 7. General Gordon
8. Al Pacino 9. *An Officer And A Gentleman* 10. *Love Me Tender*

QUIZ 251

1 According to the Scaffold song, which woman invented "medicinal compound"?

2 How old is Abba's 'Dancing Queen'?

3 In which Queen hit did Freddie Mercury say "I don't believe in Peter Pan, Frankenstein or Superman"?

4 In which song did the Stranglers ask "Whatever happened to Leon Trotsky"?

5 Which Elton John song character travelled to Spain on a plane?

6 Which 1969 Number 1 hit mentions Picasso, the Aga Khan and Marlene Dietrich in the lyrics?

7 Which Rolling Stones song character was born in a cross-fire hurricane?

8 Which Beatles song character "died in the church and was buried along with her name"?

9 Which Madonna hit mentions Gene Kelly, Fred Astaire and Jimmy Dean amongst others in the lyrics?

10 Which pop star is mentioned in the first line of lyrics of the hit 'Come On Eileen' by Dexy's Midnight Runners?

ANSWERS

1. Lily The Pink 2. 17 3. 'Bicycle Races' 4. 'No More Heroes' 5. Daniel
6. 'Where Do You Go To My Lovely?' 7. Jumpin Jack Flash 8. Eleanor Rigby
9. 'Vogue' 10. Johnny Ray

QUIZ 252

• •

1 Who is the patron saint of Wales?

2 In which song did David Bowie advise Major Tom to take a protein pill?

3 Which member of The Beatles changed his middle name from Winston to Ono?

4 Who was known as the Hammer of the Scots?

5 Who bought a controlling share of Chelsea FC in 2003?

6 In what area of Spain did Don Quixote live?

7 In which year was Prince Edward born?

8 What is the name of King Arthur's evil half-sister?

9 Who was lead vocalist for The Four Seasons?

10 Which tennis star became known as Superbrat due to his wild outbursts of temper?

ANSWERS

1. St David 2. 'Space Oddity' 3. John Lennon 4. Edward I 5. Roman Abramovich 6. La Mancha 7. 1964 8. Morgan le Fay 9. Frankie Valli 10. John McEnroe

QUIZ 253

. . . .

What is the first name of the husband in the following
TV shows?

1   Ria Parkinson's husband in *Butterflies*

2   Dorien Green's husband in *Birds Of A Feather*

3   Mary Campbell's husband in *Soap*

4   Mary Beth Lacey's husband in *Cagney And Lacey*

5   Margot Leadbetter's husband in *The Good Life*

6   Olivia Walton's husband in *The Waltons*

7   Alice Horton's husband in *The Vicar Of Dibley*

8   Yvonne Sparrow's husband in *Goodnight
    Sweetheart*

9   Sally McMillan's husband in *McMillan And Wife*

10 Brenda Hope's husband in *Auf Wiedersehen Pet*

ANSWERS

1. Ben 2. Marcus 3. Burt 4. Harvey 5. Jerry 6. John 7. Hugo 8. Gary
9. Stewart 10. Neville

QUIZ 254

• •

What is the first name of the wife in the following
   TV shows?

1 Horace Rumpole's wife in *Rumpole Of The Bailey*

2 Alf Garnett's wife in *Till Death Us Do Part*

3 Howard Cunningham's wife in *Happy Days*

4 Cliff Huxtable's wife in *The Cosby Show*

5 Reggie Perrin's wife in *The Fall And Rise Of Reginald
   Perrin*

6 Derek Trotter's wife in *Only Fools And Horses*

7 James Herriot's wife in *All Creatures Great And
   Small*

8 Gomez Addams wife in *The Addams Family*

9 Niles Crane's first wife in *Frasier*

10 Al Bundy's wife in *Married With Children*

ANSWERS

1. Hilda 2. Else 3. Marion 4. Clair 5. Elizabeth 6. Raquel 7. Helen 8. Morticia
9. Maris 10. Peggy

QUIZ 255

. . . .

Who is the patron saint of …

1 Dancers?

2 Moscow?

3 Shoemakers?

4 Television?

5 France ?

6 Tax collectors?

7 Glasgow?

8 Edinburgh?

9 Athletes?

10 Norway?

ANSWERS

1. St Vitus 2. St Boris 3. St Crispin 4. St Clare 5. St Denis 6. St Matthew
7. St Mungo 8. St Giles 9. St Sebastian 10. St Olaf

QUIZ 256

1 Who is the oldest member of the Bee Gees?

2 Which darts world champion acquired the nickname of The Power?

3 Who wears bullet-deflecting bracelets made from feminum?

4 Which song topped the charts for both Westlife and Billy Joel?

5 Who was the only Australian to be crowned Mens Singles Champion at Wimbledon in the 1980s?

6 Which world leader's autobiography is entitled *Where's The Rest Of Me*?

7 St Vincent is the patron saint of which European capital city?

8 What is the nationality of the composer Bela Bartók?

9 In which country does a train called the *William Tell Express* run?

10 In British politics, who became the leader of the Conservative Party in 1997?

ANSWERS

1. Maurice Gibb 2. Phil Taylor 3. Wonder Woman 4. Uptown Girl 5. Pat Cash
6. Ronald Reagan 7. Lisbon 8. Hungarian 9. Switzerland 10. William Hague

QUIZ 257

• •

1   In which story did Sherlock Holmes make his literary debut?

2   What is the name of the female Darling child in *Peter Pan*?

3   Which Hans Christian Andersen tale tells the story of a tiny girl discovered inside the petals of a flower?

4   Which silver screen icon's autobiography is entitled *Steps In Time*?

5   Who visited the lands of Laputa, Lilliput and Brobdingnag?

6   Which ship was captained by Captain Ahab in *Moby Dick*?

7   What is the name of Harry Potter's father?

8   During which war did Ernest Hemingway set his novel *For Whom The Bell Tolls*?

9   Which famous author had the first names of Herbert George?

10 Who partners Troilus in the title of a Shakespeare play?

ANSWERS

1. *A Study In Scarlet* 2. Wendy 3. *Thumbelina* 4. Fred Astaire 5. Gulliver
6. The *Pequod* 7. James 8. Spanish Civil War 9. HG Wells 10. Cressida

QUIZ 258

• •

1   In 1520, which British monarch met Francis I of France at The Field Of The Cloth Of Gold?

2   What is the last name of Bonnie Prince Charlie?

3   In 1993, who became the USA's first female attorney general?

4   The world's first female prime minister Sirimavo Bandaranaike became leader of which country in 1960?

5   In which city were French kings crowned prior to 1825?

6   In which year did Margaret Thatcher become Britian's first female prime minister?

7   Who was the first Plantaganet king?

8   Which famed scientist won the Nobel Prize for Physics in 1921?

9   Which native America chief had a name that means 'he makes rivers'?

10 Who was president of the USA at the outbreak of World War II?

ANSWERS

1. Henry VIII 2. Stuart 3. Janet Reno 4. Sri Lanka 5. Rheims 6. 1979 7. Henry II 8. Albert Einstein 9. Hiawatha 10. Franklin D Roosevelt

QUIZ 259

1 Which pop star and actress sang 'Hopelessly Devoted To You' in the film *Grease*?

2 What is the subtitle of the 2003 film sequel *X Men II*?

3 The 1989 film *The Delinquents* marked the big screen debut of which former *Neighbours* star?

4 In which 1987 film did Jack Nicholson portray a personification of the Devil?

5 Who played the title role in the 1994 film *Ed Wood*?

6 What was the title of the first film in which Harrison Ford played the CIA operative Jack Ryan?

7 In which film did Hugh Grant play a bookshop owner who falls in love with Julia Roberts?

8 Which film character is associated with the phrase "Go ahead, make my day"?

9 Who is the mother of Jamie Lee Curtis?

10 Which is the home city of Rocky Balboa?

ANSWERS

1. Olivia Newton John 2. *X Men United* 3. Kylie Minogue 4. *The Witches Of Eastwick* 5. Johnny Depp 6. *Patriot Games* 7. *Notting Hill* 8. *Dirty Harry* 9. Janet Leigh 10. Philadelphia

QUIZ 260

1 Who, born Gladys Smith, was a founder member of United Artists?

2 Who played the title role in *Billy Elliot*?

3 In which 1998 film did Leonardo Di Caprio play twin brothers?

4 Which 1957 film saw Alec Guinness marching to the whistled tune of 'Colonel Bogey'?

5 Which singer was portrayed by Sissy Spacek in *Coal Miner's Daughter*?

6 Who played Anakin Skywalker in *Star Wars: Attack Of The Clones*?

7 In which film did Bruce Willis voice the character of Mikey?

8 What did the actor Christian Hawkins change his last name to?

9 Who played the leading man of Julie Andrews in *The Sound Of Music*?

10 Which actor was the travelling companion of Steve Martin in *Planes, Trains And Automobiles*?

ANSWERS

1. Mary Pickford 2. Jamie Bell 3. *The Man In The Iron Mask* 4. *Bridge On The River Kwai* 5. Loretta Lynn 6. Hayden Christiansen 7. *Look Who's Talking* 8. Slater 9. Christopher Plummer 10. John Candy

QUIZ 261

• •

The answers to the following ten questions all contain the names Peter, Paul or Mary.

1 Who left the rock group Genesis and later had hit solo albums entitled *Us* and *Up*?

2 Who drove the car in which Princess Diana was killed?

3 Who founded her own production company called MTM?

4 Who played the evil Grand Moff Tarkin in *Star Wars*?

5 Which French-born artist was portrayed by Anthony Quinn in the film *Lust For Life*?

6 Who wrote the novel *Frankenstein*?

7 Who was the first actor to win a posthumous Best Actor Oscar?

8 Who married his *Crocodile Dundee* co-star Linda Kozlowski in 1990?

9 In 1990, who became the first female president of the Republic of Ireland?

10 Which actor's most famous role is that of the scruffy detective Columbo?

ANSWERS

1.Peter Gabriel 2.Henri Paul 3.Mary Tyler Moore 4.Peter Cushing 5.Paul Gauguin 6.Mary Shelley 7.Peter Finch 8.Paul Hogan 9.Mary Robinson 10. Peter Falk

QUIZ 262

1. Who is the Roman goddess of hunting?

2. Who was president of the USA throughout World War I?

3. Which female singer did Elton John collaborate with on his first chart-topping single?

4. On which Caribbean island was the cricket star Brian Lara born?

5. Which year saw the tears of Paul Gascoine in a World Cup semi final?

6. Which song was a hit for the Bee Gees in 1968 and later a hit for Boyzone in 1996?

7. In which month is St George's Day?

8. Dave, Noddy, Jimmy and Don comprised which glam rock group?

9. In which year did Cassius Clay win an Olympic gold medal?

10. Which rock group named themselves after the inventor of the seed drill?

ANSWERS

1. Diana 2. Woodrow Wilson 3. Kiki Dee 4. Trinidad 5. 1990 6. 'Words'
7. April 8. Slade 9. 1960 10. Jethro Tull

QUIZ 263

In which TV show did …

1 Richard Briers play Martin Bryce?

2 Doug McClure play Trampas?

3 Patrick McGoohan play Number Six?

4 Kirstie Alley play Veronica Chase Anderson?

5 Stephen Fry play Lord Melchett?

6 Jasper Carrott play Bob Louis?

7 Angus Deayton play Patrick Trench?

8 Robert Vaughan play Harry Rule?

9 Linda Robson play Tracey Stubbs?

10 David Jason play Ted Simcock?

ANSWERS

1. *Ever Decreasing Circles* 2. *The Virginian* 3. *The Prisoner* 4. *Veronica's Closet*
5. *Blackadder II* 6. *The Detectives* 7. *One Foot In The Grave* 8. *The Protectors*
9. *Birds Of A Feather* 10. *A Bit Of A Do*

QUIZ 264

• •

1 Which short-sighted cartoon hero has two nephews called Waldo and Prezley?

2 In which series does Caroline Aherne play Denise Best?

3 Who played the title role in *Spenser For Hire*?

4 Who is the archenemy of Dangermouse?

5 What type of bird did Dastardly and Muttley attempt to capture in their flying machines?

6 Which dim-witted character is played by Roger Lloyd Pack in *Only Fools And Horses*?

7 In *Stingray*, who owned a pet seal called Oink?

8 Who is the archenemy of Captain Pugwash?

9 In which city was *The Boys From The Black Stuff* set?

10 In which cult series did David Dixon play Ford Prefect?

ANSWERS

1. Mr Magoo 2. *The Royle Family* 3. Robert Urich 4. Baron Greenback
5. Pigeon 6. Trigger 7. Marina 8. Cut Throat Jake 9. Liverpool 10. *The Hitchhiker's Guide To The Galaxy*

QUIZ 265

• •

What do the middle initials of the following people stand for?

1   Ian T Botham

2   Richard M Nixon

3   Thomas A Edison

4   William J Hague

5   Hugh M Grant

6   James T Kirk

7   Lyndon B Johnson

8   George W Bush

9   Gary W Lineker

10   John F Kennedy

ANSWERS

1. Terence 2. Milhouse 3. Alva 4. Jefferson 5. Mungo 6. Tiberius 7. Baines
8. Walker 9. Winston 10. Fitzgerald

QUIZ 266

. . . .

What are the first names of the following duos?

1 Morecambe and Wise

2 Simon and Garfunkel

3 Rodgers and Hammerstein

4 The Everly Brothers

5 Alcock and Brown

6 The Righteous Brothers

7 Abbot and Costello

8 Jekyll and Hyde

9 Cannon and Ball

10 Dempsey and Makepeace

ANSWERS

1. Eric and Ernie 2. Paul and Art 3. Richard and Oscar 4. Phil and Don
5. John and Arthur 6. Bill and Bobby 7. Lou and Bud 8. Henry and Edward
9. Tommy and Bobby 10. James and Harriet

QUIZ 267

• •

1   How are Roberta, Phyllis and Peter collectively
    known in the title of a novel by E Nesbit?

2   Who created the equine hero Black Beauty?

3   What is the home town of Dr Doolittle?

4   *Billy Budd* was the last novel of which author?

5   Who wrote her first novel, *Mrs Dalloway*, in 1925
    and committed suicide 16 years later?

6   Which French author was granted a national
    funeral in 1885 and buried in the Pantheon?

7   In which century was Lord Byron born?

8   Which of the Brontë sisters died from tubercolosis
    in 1849?

9   Who wrote the words to the song 'Auld Lang
    Syne'?

10 What was the title of the second book to feature
    the character of Winnie The Pooh?

ANSWERS

1. The Railway Children 2. Anna Sewell 3. Puddleby-On-Marsh 4. Herman
Melville 5. Virginia Woolf 6. Victor Hugo 7. 18th 8. Anne Brontë 9. Robert
Burns 10. *The House At Pooh Corner*

QUIZ 268

• •

1 Which former US president was the recipient of the Nobel Peace Prize in 2002?

2 Whose last recording before his death in 1959 was the song 'It Doesn't Matter Anymore'?

3 In 1830 which religious leader published the book entitled *The Book Of Mormon*?

4 In 1521 who defined his religious beliefs at the Diet Of Worms?

5 Which country was ruled in the 1400s by King Ferdinand V?

6 In which decade did Chanel No 5 perfume first go on sale?

7 Who commanded the Mexican troops at the Battle of the Alamo?

8 How many queens have ruled France?

9 Which instrument was Glenn Miller known for playing?

10 Whose tombstone bears the inscription "Workers of all lands unite"?

ANSWERS

1.Jimmy Carter 2.Buddy Holly 3. Joseph Smith 4.Martin Luther 5. Spain
6. 1920s 7. General Santa Ana 8. None 9. Trombone 10. Karl Marx

QUIZ 269

1 Which actor played the hero in the films *Juggernaut* and *Camelot*?

2 In which film did Meryl Streep play the role of Karen Blixen?

3 Who played Joe Black in the 1998 film *Meet Joe Black*?

4 Which star of the film *Live And Let Die* was born Joyce Frankenberg?

5 In which classic movie did Orson Welles play the role of Harry Lime?

6 Which actor played the LA cop Billy Rosewood in *Beverly Hills Cop*?

7 In which film, based on a true story, did Robert Redford play the governor of Wakefield Prison Farm?

8 In which 1999 film did Johnny Depp attempt to solve the mystery of a headless horseman?

9 In which film did Frank Sinatra sing 'Who Wants To Be A Millionaire'?

10 Which actress was nicknamed The Divine Sarah?

ANSWERS

1. Richard Harris 2. *Out Of Africa* 3. Brad Pitt 4. Jane Seymour 5. *The Third Man* 6. Judge Reinhold 7. *Brubaker* 8. *Sleepy Hollow* 9. *High Society* 10. Sarah Bernhardt

QUIZ 270

• •

1 In which film did Frankie Avalon sing 'Beauty School Dropout'?

2 Which role was played by Alec Guinness in the 1948 version of *Oliver Twist*?

3 Who played the title role in the 2002 film *The Adventures Of Pluto Nash*?

4 What is the nationality of film star Heath Ledger?

5 Who did Judi Dench portray in the film *Mrs Brown*?

6 Which hoofed Disney hero was created by Felix Salten?

7 Who provided the speaking voice of Jessica Rabbit?

8 Who played the role of M in the Bond movie *Never Say Never Again*?

9 On which movie star's book was the film *Postcards From The Edge* based?

10 What were Indiana Jones and his father searching for in *Indiana Jones And The Last Crusade*?

ANSWERS

1. *Grease* 2. Fagin 3. Eddie Murphy 4. Australian 5. Queen Victoria 6. Bambi
7. Kathleen Turner 8. Edward Fox 9. Carrie Fisher 10. The Holy Grail

QUIZ 271

. . . .

The following ten answers all contain the name of Tom, Dick or Harry.

1   Which author created the CIA agent Jack Ryan?

2   In 1975 who, at the age of 34, was appointed chief-of-staff in the US government?

3   Which entertainer was knighted in 1981 and later penned the autobiography *Arias And Raspberries*?

4   Who played the Greek lover of Pauline Collins in *Shirley Valentine*?

5   At the 1968 Summer Olympics, who gave his name to a new style of high jump?

6   Who was the 33rd president of the USA?

7   Who links the films *Quigley Down Under* and *Three Men And A Baby*?

8   Who was first appointed lord mayor of London in 1397?

9   Who was born Ehrich Weiss in March 1874?

10 Which playwright penned the screenplay for the Oscar winning film *Shakespeare In Love*?

ANSWERS

1. Tom Clancy 2. Dick Cheney 3. Harry Secombe 4. Tom Conti 5. Dick Fosbury 6. Harry S Truman 7. Tom Selleck 8. Dick Whittington 9. Harry Houdini 10. Tom Stoppard

QUIZ 272

1 As a baby, by what name was Superman known?

2 Which Italian football star scored the only goal in the 2000 FA Cup final?

3 Which military rank is held by James Bond?

4 Who duetted with Olivia Newton John on the song 'Summer Nights'?

5 Which Spice Girl wrote an autobiography entitled *If Only*?

6 Who won Olympic gold medals in 1980 and 1984 for the 1500 metres?

7 Who founded Wham with George Michael?

8 Which Italian club did Paul Gascoine play for?

9 Who is the drummer for the Rolling Stones?

10 Which boxer lost the Thriller In Manila?

ANSWERS

1. Kal-El 2. Roberto Di Matteo 3. Commander 4. John Travolta 5. Geri Halliwell 6. Sebastian Coe 7. Andrew Ridgeley 8. Lazio 9. Charlie Watts 10. Joe Frazier

QUIZ 273

. . . .

Which TV shows feature the following groups
   of children?

1   Bart, Lisa and Maggie

2   Jenny and David Porter

3   Adam, Hoss and Little Joe

4   Katie and Tom Pottage

5   Darlene, Becky and DJ

6   Laura, Mary, Carrie and Nellie

7   Tabitha Stephens

8   Kelly and Bud Bundy

9   Arnold, Willis and Kimberly Drummond

10 Brains, Sticks, Scooper, Tiger, Doughnut and Billie

ANSWERS

1. *The Simpsons* 2. *2.4 Children* 3. *Bonanza* 4. *Postman Pat* 5. *Roseanne*
6. *Little House On The Prairie* 7. *Bewitched* 8. *Married With Children*
9. *Diff'rent Strokes* 10. *Here Come The Double Deckers*

QUIZ 274

• •

1 Which series first featured the alien character of Mork?

2 What was the nationality of the secret agent played by David McCallum in *The Man From U.N.C.L.E.*?

3 In which crime drama does Geraldine Somerville play DS Jane Penhaligon?

4 On which beach does Mitch Buchannon work as a lifeguard in *Baywatch*?

5 Who played the 1970s TV detective Harry O?

6 In which TV sequel did Ronnie Barker reprise his role of Norman Stanley Fletcher?

7 Who played DCI Slater in *Only Fools And Horses* and went on to become an Oscar-winning actor?

8 Which Avenger was played by Honor Blackman?

9 What is the daytime job of Lieutenant Corporal Jones in *Dad's Army*?

10 The Cylons were alien villains in which sci-fi TV series?

ANSWERS

QUIZ 275

1 Which pop music icon was shot dead outside a New York building called The Dakota?

2 By which four-letter name is the rock hero Paul Hewson better known?

3 Which soul legend collaborated with George Michael on the hit record *I Knew You Were Waiting*?

4 Which ZS is an alter ego of David Bowie?

5 Who has had hits collaborating with Tina Turner, Jeff Beck and the Scotland World Cup Squad?

6 Which cult hero was portayed by Val Kilmer in the film *The Doors*?

7 Who has the middle names of Veronica Louise and the last name of Ciccone?

8 In which film did Elvis Presley sing 'Wooden Heart'?

9 Which year marked the death of Freddie Mercury?

10 In which song were Paul McCartney and Stevie Wonder "living together in perfect harmony"?

ANSWERS

1. John Lennon 2. Bono 3. Aretha Franklin 4. Ziggy Stardust 5. Rod Stewart
6. Jim Morrison 7. Madonna 8. *GI Blues* 9. 1991 10. 'Ebony And Ivory'

QUIZ 276

• •

Are the following statements fact or fib?

1 The last queen of Sweden was called Ulrika.

2 Queen Elizabeth I had a morbid fear of roses.

3 St Apollonia is the patron saint of gravediggers.

4 Only one US president has been a bachelor.

5 Cliff Richard is the grandson of the Channel swimmer Captain Webb.

6 Before finding fame as a movie star Clark Gable worked as a lumberjack.

7 The pop star Sting was given his stage name because he once worked as a beekeeper.

8 Bondi Beach in Australia was named after a surfer called James Bondi.

9 Attila the Hun bled to death on his wedding night from a nose bleed.

10 The actor Daniel Day Lewis is the son-in-law of the playwright Arthur Miller.

ANSWERS

1. Fact 2. Fact 3. Fib (the patron saint of dentists) 4. Fact (James Buchanan)
5. Fib 6. Fact 7. Fib (it was after a yellow-and-black striped jumper he wore)
8. Fib 9. Fact 10. Fact

QUIZ 277

· ·

1 What is the name of the rival family of the Montagues in *Romeo And Juliet*?

2 How many children comprise Enid Blyton's Famous Five?

3 On which thoroughfare does Harry Potter live with the Dursleys?

4 Archdeacon Frollo is the villain in which novel?

5 Whose famed poem 'The Raven' was published in 1845?

6 Which duo ate slices of quince with a runcible spoon?

7 Whose death is chronicled in the TS Eliot play *Murder In The Cathedral*?

8 What is the home county of the literary hero Ross Poldark?

9 What is the occupation of Mr McGregor in the Beatrix Potter tales?

10 *The Gremlins* was the first children's story penned by which author?

ANSWERS

1. Capulet 2. Four children and Timmy the dog 3. Privet Drive 4. *The Hunchback Of Notre Dame* 5. Edgar Allan Poe 6. 'The Owl And The Pussycat' 7. Thomas Becket 8. Cornwall 9. Farmer 10. Roald Dahl

QUIZ 278

. . . .

1 Name either of the two centuries in which Leonardo da Vinci was alive.

2 Who succeeded George Washington as president of the USA?

3 Who invented the revolver in 1835?

4 What name was given to the Polish trade union led by Lech Walesa?

5 On which island did Queen Victoria die?

6 What did Shadrach escape from in the Bible?

7 Which native American tribe was led by Geronimo?

8 For how many days did Lady Jane Grey rule?

9 In which decade did Alexander Graham Bell invent the telephone?

10 Which British monarch died in 1936?

ANSWERS

1. 15th or 16th 2. John Adams 3. Samuel Colt 4. Solidarity 5. Isle of Wight
6. The fiery furnace 7. Apache 8. Nine days 9. 1870s 10. George V

QUIZ 279

- -

1   Who played Jor-El, the father of Superman in the 1978 movie?

2   Who played Lex Luthor's bumbling sidekick in the *Superman* movies?

3   What was the sub-title of the fourth *Superman* movie?

4   What colour is the letter S on Superman's costume?

5   Who played a computer expert called Gus Gorman in *Superman III*?

6   Which newspaper editor is portrayed in the *Superman* movies by Jackie Cooper?

7   What element is Superman unable to penetrate with his x-ray vision?

8   Who played Lara, the mother of Superman in the 1978 film?

9   Which employee of the *Daily Planet* was played by Marc McClure?

10 Which super villain was created by Lex Luthor in *Superman IV*?

ANSWERS

1. Marlon Brando 2. Ned Beatty 3. *The Quest For Peace* 4. Red 5. Richard Pryor 6. Perry White 7. Lead 8. Susannah York 9. Jimmy Olsen 10. Nuclear Man

QUIZ 280

1 What is the name of Rocky Balboa's wife?

2 Which director links the films *Minority Report*, *Always* and *Saving Private Ryan*?

3 Who played Gunner Sergeant Emil Foley in *An Officer And A Gentleman*?

4 Who was born Leonard Slye and went on to become known as The King of the Cowboys?

5 In which film did Ed Norton play a priest called Brian Finn and Ben Stiller play a rabbi called Jake Schram?

6 In which film did Haley Joel Osment play a robotic child called David?

7 Which decade did Michael J Fox travel back to in the 1985 film *Back To The Future*?

8 Whose final film as a director was entitled *Family Plot*?

9 Which comedy actor played the title role in *The Man With Two Brains*?

10 Who plays a female villain called Madison Lee in the 2003 film *Charlie's Angels:Full Throttle*?

ANSWERS

1. Adrian 2. Steven Spielberg 3. Louis Gossett Jnr 4. Roy Rogers 5. *Keeping The Faith* 6. *A.I.* 7. 1950s 8. Alfred Hitchcock 9. Steve Martin 10. Demi Moore

QUIZ 281

. . . .

1   Which eye-patch wearing star of the 1960s was backed by The Pirates?

2   Who backed Martha Reeves on the song 'Dancing In The Street'?

3   Who accompanied The Waves when winning the Eurovision Song Contest?

4   Who caught a 'Midnight Train To Georgia' with The Pips?

5   By what name was Declan McManus better known when backed by The Attractions?

6   Which rock legend had a hit with the song 'Layla' under the guise of Derek And The Dominoes?

7   Which 1980s pop star was backed by The Coconuts?

8   Who was backed by The Dakotas on the number one hit 'Little Children'?

9   Which eccentric rock star received backing from The Mothers Of Invention?

10 Which 1960s chart topper was backed by The Shondells?

ANSWERS

1. Johnny Kidd 2. The Vandellas 3. Katrina 4. Gladys Knight 5. Elvis Costello
6. Eric Clapton 7. Kid Creole 8. Billy J Kramer 9. Frank Zappa 10. Tommy
James

QUIZ 282

. . . .

1   According to the Bible who said "Forgive them
    Father, for they know not what they do"?

2   Which prime minister claimed there would be
    peace in our time after pledging to the Munich
    Agreement?

3   Which boxer lost The Rumble In The Jungle?

4   How old was Elvis Presley when he died?

5   Was the original name of Mickey Mouse,
    Marmaduke, Morrisey or Mortimer?

6   Which rock and roll legend was born Richard
    Penniman?

7   Which US marine colonel was at the centre of the
    Irangate scandal?

8   What kind of animal raised Romulus and Remus?

9   Which superhero works under an assumed
    identity as a photographer for the *Daily Bugle*?

10 Who was the subject of the Don McLean hit
    'Vincent'?

ANSWERS

1. Jesus Christ 2. Neville Chamberlain 3. George Foreman 4. 42 5. Mortimer
6. Little Richard 7. Colonel Oliver North 8. Wolf 9. Spiderman 10. Vincent
Van Gogh

QUIZ 283

• •

Which *Star Trek* characters are played by the
    following actors?

1 Walter Koenig

2 Patrick Stewart

3 DeForest Kelley

4 Brent Spiner

5 George Takei

6 Gates McFadden

7 Scott Bakula

8 Leonard Nimoy

9 Majel Barrett

10 Wil Weaton

ANSWERS

1. Ensign Pavel Checkov 2. Captain Jean Luc Picard 3. Dr Leonard "Bones"
McCoy 4. Lieutenant Commander Data 5. Mr Sulu 6. Dr Beverley Crusher
7. Captain Jonathan Archer 8. Mr Spock 9. Nurse Christine Chapel
10. Wesley Crusher

QUIZ 284

1 In *The Simpsons*, what colour is Marge Simpson's hair?

2 Which classic comedy series includes episodes entitled *Gourmet Night* and *The Germans*?

3 In which TV series does Robson Green play the role of Dr Tony Hill?

4 Which trio of bears live at Wonderland Zoo?

5 Who played the title role in *Remmington Steele*?

6 In which city does Joe Friday bring criminals to justice in *Dragnet*?

7 Which colonel was rebuilt by Dr Rudy Wells?

8 By what six-letter name is Hiram Hackenbacker otherwise known in *Thunderbirds*?

9 Which literary creation of Dorothy L Sayers was played on TV by Ian Carmichael?

10 William, Patrick, Jon, Tom, Peter, Colin, Sylvester and Paul. What is the connection?

ANSWERS

1. Blue 2. *Fawlty Towers* 3. *Wire In The Blood* 4. The Hair Bear Bunch
5. Pierce Brosnan 6. Los Angeles 7. Colonel Steve Austin, the Bionic Man
8. Brains 9. Lord Peter Wimsey 10. First names of actors who have played Dr Who

QUIZ 285

1 On which record label did The Beatles have their first hit in 1962?

2 Which pop superstar returned to the album charts in 2001 with *Songs From The West Coast*?

3 Which singing siblings provided Stock, Aitken and Waterman with their first number one hit as producers?

4 The video for which song saw Adam Ant dressed as a dandy highwayman?

5 Who, born Ernest Evans, later became known as The King Of Twist?

6 Which member of the Traveling Wilburys died in December 1988?

7 Who provides lead vocals for the pop group Blondie?

8 In what year did Robbie Williams make an acrimonious split from Take That?

9 On which island was Freddie Mercury born?

10 Who was the subject of the Sting hit record 'An Englishman In New York'?

ANSWERS

1. Parlephone 2. Elton John 3. Mel and Kim 4. *Stand And Deliver*
5. Chubby Checker 6. Roy Orbison 7. Debbie Harry 8. 1995 9. Zanzibar
10. Quentin Crisp

QUIZ 286

• •

1. Which half of a famous double act was born Arthur Jefferson?

2. Which country and western singer founded the band The First Edition?

3. After which god was the month of March named?

4. What was the first number one hit for Rod Stewart?

5. Which trade union for actors was founded by Dame May Whitty?

6. Which song did Celine Dion record as the theme for the blockbuster movie *Titanic*?

7. Which sporting hero was born in 1895, died in 1948 and had the real first names of George Herman?

8. What kind of bird was Florence Nightingale said to have carried around in her pocket?

9. John Fairfax was the first person to row solo across which body of water?

10. Which song topped the UK charts for Elvis Presley, shortly after his death?

ANSWERS

1. Stan Laurel 2. Kenny Rogers 3. Mars 4. 'Maggie May' 5. Equity
6. 'My Heart Will Go On' 7. Babe Ruth 8. An owl 9. The Atlantic Ocean
10. 'Way Down'

QUIZ 287

1. In which city was *The Prime Of Miss Jean Brodie* set?

2. Who is the longest holder of the title of poet laureate?

3. In *Pygmalion*, which professor lives on Wimpole Street?

4. According to the author Arthur Conan Doyle, in which county was Sherlock Holmes born?

5. *White Cap And Balls* is the title of the autobiography of which cricket umpire?

6. Who created the literary heroine Lorna Doone?

7. Which fictional hero died at Fort Zinderneuf?

8. Who penned the novel *Journey To The Centre Of The Earth*?

9. Which pop star shares his name with a literary hero created by Henry Fielding?

10. In which town is William Shakespeare buried?

ANSWERS

1. Edinburgh 2. Alfred Lord Tennyson 3. Henry Higgins 4. Yorkshire
5. Dickie Bird 6. RD Blackmore 7. Beau Geste 8. Jules Verne 9. Tom Jones
10. Straford Upon Avon

QUIZ 288

1 Montezuma II was the last emperor of which ancient race?

2 Who was the youngest person to become president of the USA?

3 Who was appointed president of the Screen Actors Guild in 1947 and later became US president?

4 In which building was the body of Horatio Nelson interred?

5 Who became the first woman to fly across the Atlantic Ocean?

6 At which town did Harold II lose the Battle Of Hastings?

7 Who was crowned queen of England in January 1559?

8 Whose impeachment trial began in January 1999?

9 Who was the first person to see Jesus after his resurrection?

10 Who was created empress of India in 1877?

ANSWERS

1. Aztecs 2. Theodore Roosevelt 3. Ronald Reagan 4. St Paul's Cathedral
5. Amelia Earhart 6. Battle 7. Queen Elizabeth I 8. Bill Clinton 9. Mary
Magdalene 10. Queen Victoria

QUIZ 289

1 Who played Agent J in *Men In Black*?

2 In which futuristic thriller did Harrison Ford play a bounty hunter called Rick Deckard?

3 Who played the title role in the 1995 film *Judge Dredd*?

4 Who plays the role of Polly Prince in the 2004 film *Along Came Polly*?

5 In which film did Paul Newman play an alcoholic lawyer called Frank Galvin?

6 Who played Danny Ocean in the 2001 film remake of *Ocean's Eleven*?

7 Who won a Best Director Oscar for the film *Titanic*?

8 Which 2000 film saw Tom Hanks attempting to survive on a desert island?

9 Who plays the role of Jason Bourne in the 2002 action thriller *The Bourne Identity*?

10 In which 1990 film did Michael Keaton play the deranged lodger of Matthew Modine?

ANSWERS

1. Will Smith 2. *Blade Runner* 3. Sylvester Stallone 4. Jennifer Aniston 5. *The Verdict* 6. George Clooney 7. James Cameron 8. *Cast Away* 9. Matt Damon 10. *Pacific Heights*

QUIZ 290

1. Who won a Best Actor Oscar for his role in the film *The Goodbye Girl*?

2. Who played the role of Papa Thorson in his last big screen appearance in the movie *The Hunter*?

3. Who played Mozart in the Oscar-winning film *Amadeus*?

4. In which 1992 film did Tom Cruise face Jack Nicholson in a court room?

5. Who played the flat mate of Walter Matthau in the film comedy *The Odd Couple*?

6. Which Wookie is the co-pilot of Han Solo?

7. Jack Palance, Danny De Vito and Michelle Pfeiffer have all played villains in which series of films?

8. Who played the role of Carrie White in the 1976 film *Carrie*?

9. Who played the role of Storm in the 2000 film *X Men*?

10. In the TV cop drama *NYPD Blue*, which tragic character lost a wife, a son and two partners?

ANSWERS

1. Richard Dreyfus 2. Steve McQueen 3. Tom Hulce 4. *A Few Good Men*
5. Jack Lemmon 6. Chewbacca 7. Batman 8. Sissy Spacek 9. Halle Berry
10. Andy Sipowicz

QUIZ 291

1 Who is the known as The Father of Frozen Food?

2 In 1765 who invented the steam engine condensor?

3 Who gave his name to the airship that he invented in 1900?

4 In which decade did Christopher Cockerell invent the hovercraft?

5 Which artificial language was invented by Dr Zamenhof?

6 Which gaming device was invented by Blaise Pascal while conducting experiments into perpetual motion?

7 Who invented dynamite before giving his name to a series of prizes?

8 Which French brothers invented the hot-air balloon?

9 Who received a knighthood after inventing the jet engine?

10 What links the inventions of the bunsen burner, the Rubik's cube and the biro pen?

ANSWERS

1. Clarence Birdseye 2. James Watt 3. Ferdinand Von Zeppelin 4. 1950s
5. Esperanto 6. Roulette wheel 7. Alfred Nobel 8. Montgolfier Brothers
9. Sir Frank Whittle 10. All were named after their inventors

QUIZ 292

• •

1   How did Captain Hook lose his hand in *Peter Pan*?

2   In which month of the year is St David's Day?

3   Under which name did Declan McManus carve out a pop career?

4   Who is the youngest of the Three Tenors?

5   Who served as secretary of state for Richard Nixon?

6   Which boxer acquired the nickname of, The Punching Preacher in his comeback fights?

7   Which Welsh born singer was backed by The Sunsets?

8   Which US state was named after Queen Elizabeth I?

9   Marduk was the supreme god of which civilization's mythology?

10 What is the four-letter name of the supermodel who tied the knot with David Bowie?

ANSWERS

1. Bitten off by a crocodile 2. March 3. Elvis Costello 4. José Carreras
5. Henry Kissinger 6. George Foreman 7. Shakin' Stevens 8. Virginia (from
the Virgin Queen) 9. Babylonian 10. Iman

QUIZ 293

. . . .

1　In *Thunderbirds*, what is the registration plate of Lady Penelope's pink Rolls Royce?

2　Who played the role of Lucas McCain in the 1960s TV western *The Rifleman*?

3　Which of Batman's foes is the leader of the Molehill Mob?

4　What colour is Klingon blood?

5　Which role was played by Richard Anderson in *The Six Million Dollar Man*?

6　What is the first name of *A Man Called Ironside*?

7　Which TV character is assisted by Tinker, Eric and Beth?

8　Whom did David Suchet protray when living at 203 Whitehaven Mansions?

9　In which series did DI Maggie Forbes work at Seven Dials police station?

10　In which crime drama did James Grout play Chief Superintendant Strange?

ANSWERS

1. FAB 1　2. Chuck Connors　3. The Riddler　4. Purple　5. Oscar Goldman
6. Robert　7. Lovejoy　8. Hercule Poirot　9. *The Gentle Touch*　10. *Inspector Morse*

QUIZ 294

Who played the role of…

1 Detective Danny Sorenson in *NYPD Blue*?

2 Rowdy Yates in *Rawhide*?

3 Detective Lieutenant Mike Stone in *The Streets Of San Francisco*?

4 DI Jack Regan in *The Sweeney*?

5 Jim Phelps in *Mission Impossible*?

6 Michael Knight in *Knight Rider*?

7 Jonathan Smith in *Highway To Heaven*?

8 Rene Artois in *Allo Allo*?

9 Captain Frank Furillo in *Hill Street Blues*?

10 Agent Dale Cooper in *Twin Peaks*?

ANSWERS

1. Rick Schroder 2. Clint Eastwood 3. Karl Malden 4. John Thaw 5. Peter Graves 6. David Hasselhoff 7. Michael Landon 8. Gorden Kaye 9. Daniel Travanti 10. Kyle MacLachlan

QUIZ 295

• •

1 In 2002 who was the last member of The Goons to die?

2 Which comedy curmudgeon's catchphrase is "I don't believe it"?

3 What is the occupation of Simon Sparrow in a series of British comedy films?

4 Which British comedian who died in 1993 penned the autobiography *A Clown Too Many*?

5 Brian Potter is the lead character in which comedy series?

6 Who first appeared as The Vicar Of Dibley in 1994?

7 In which country was the *Carry On* star Sid James born?

8 In which London borough did the Trotter family live in a tower block called Nelson Mandela House?

9 What is 'the Fonz' short for in *Happy Days*?

10 In which series did Don Estelle play Lofty Sugden?

ANSWERS

QUIZ 296

. . . .

1 Who is the brother of Zeus and the god of the sea?

2 Who was appointed US secretary of state in 2000?

3 How many members of Abba were Swedish?

4 Kim Campbell became the first female prime minister of which country in 1993?

5 Who recorded the albums *Faith* and *Older*?

6 Which of the Four Horsemen of the Apocalypse rides a pale horse?

7 Which US president was nicknamed The Comeback Kid?

8 Which Andrew Lloyd Webber musical features trains called Bobo, Electra and Rusty?

9 Who recorded the best-selling album *Songs In The Key Of Life*?

10 Which planet shares its name with the Greek god of the underworld?

ANSWERS

1. Poseidon 2. Colin Powell 3. Three 4. Canada 5. George Michael 6. Death
7. Bill Clinton 8. *Starlight Express* 9. Stevie Wonder 10. Pluto

QUIZ 297

1. What type of headgear is favoured by Sherlock Holmes?

2. What was the title of the Cliff Richard stage musical based on the novel *Wuthering Heights*?

3. What is the name of Othello's wife in the Shakespeare play?

4. Which film starring Linda Blair was based on a novel by William Peter Blatty?

5. What kind of bird did the Ancient Mariner shoot dead?

6. In a nursery rhyme, whose pocket is found by Kitty Fisher?

7. Which novel by Charles Kingsley features the central character of Tom the chimney sweep?

8. What kind of animal is the literary character Tarka?

9. Which novel by Roddy Doyle, later filmed, told the story of an Irish soul band?

10. Which doctor created by Max Brand was played on TV by Richard Chamberlain?

ANSWERS

1. Deerstalker 2. Heathcliff 3. Desdemona 4. *The Exorcist* 5. Albatross
6. Lucy Lockett 7. *The Water Babies* 8. Otter 9. *The Commitments*
10. Dr Kildare

QUIZ 298

. . . .

1 Which US president abolished slavery?

2 Which Russian is supposed to have said" A single death is a tragedy, a million deaths is a statistic"?

3 Which organization was awarded the Nobel Peace Prize in 1917 and 1944?

4 Who was secretary general of the UN from 1972 to 1982?

5 According to Greek mythology, who was the first woman on Earth?

6 Whose brutal Khmer Rouge regime was overthrown in 1979?

7 Which governor of Judea ordered the death of Jesus Christ?

8 Which British monarch played in the Wimbledon championships in 1926?

9 Manuel II was the last monarch of which European country?

10 In 1999 which country voted to re-elect Queen Elizabeth II as their head of state?

ANSWERS

QUIZ 299

. . . .

Identify ten films from their lead hero and chief villain.

1 1991 Clarice Starling and Hannibal Lecter

2 1995 John McClane and Simon Gruber

3 1994 Jack Traven and Howard Payne

4 1981 Indiana Jones and Dr Rene Belloq

5 1987 Sergeant Martin Riggs and Mr Joshua

6 1967 Baloo and Shere Khan

7 1984 Axel Foley and Victor Maitland

8 1995 The Mariner and The Deacon

9 2000 Maximus and Commodus

10 1991 Dr Richard Kimble and Dr Charles Nichols

ANSWERS

1. *Silence Of The Lambs* 2. *Die Hard With A Vengence* 3. *Speed* 4. *Raiders Of The Lost Ark* 5. *Lethal Weapon* 6. *The Jungle Book* 7. *Beverly Hills Cop* 8. *Waterworld* 9. *Gladiator* 10. *The Fugitive*

QUIZ 300

In which city were the following film stars born?

1 Was Marlene Dietrich born in Munich, Berlin or Hamburg?

2 Was Keanu Reeves born in Beirut, Baghdad or Bratislava?

3 Was Dan Aykroyd born in Toronto, Ottawa or Quebec?

4 Was Cary Grant born in Birmingham, Glasgow or Bristol?

5 Was Judi Dench born in York, Liverpool or Manchester?

6 Was Charlie Chaplin born in Paris, New York or London?

7 Was Kenneth Branagh born in Cardiff, Belfast or Edinburgh?

8 Was Richard Attenborough born in Oxford, Cambridge or Durham?

9 Was Audrey Hepburn born in Amsterdam, Brussels or Madrid?

10 Was Britt Ekland born in Stockholm, Oslo or Helsinki?

ANSWERS

1. Berlin 2. Beirut 3. Ottawa 4. Bristol 5. York 6. London 7. Belfast
8. Cambridge 9. Brussels 10. Stockholm